STUDY GUIDE

Janda / Berry / Goldman / Hula

The Challenge of Democracy

Brief Edition

SIXTH EDITION

Melissa A. Butler

Wabash College

Updated by

Kevin W. Hula

Loyola College in Maryland

HOUGHTON MIFFLIN COMPANY BOSTON NEW YORK

Sponsoring Editor: *Katherine Meisenheimer*
Development Editor: *Jeff Greene*
Editorial Assistant: *Kristen Craib*
Editorial Assistant: *Michelle O'Berg*
Executive Marketing Manager: *Nicola Poser*
Marketing Associate: *Kathleen Mellon*

Printed in the U.S.A.

ISBN: 0-618-50366-8

3456789-VH-10 09 08

Contents

Introduction

So, you've decided to take a course in American government! Perhaps you are planning a career in politics or government. For you, this course may be a step on the road to a major in political science. Or you may have enrolled in the class because you need another social science course to meet the graduation requirements at your college or university. Or you might be somewhere in the middle, a student who is a good citizen and wants to learn more about how American government and politics work.

This study guide is for people in these three groups. Basically, the study guide is designed to help you fulfill the following four purposes:

1. To help you brush up on some of the learning skills useful in understanding American government or political science in general.

2. To reinforce what you have learned through your reading of *The Challenge of Democracy*, Brief Edition.

3. To introduce you to various reference works and data sources that may be useful to you as a political scientist or as a citizen.

4. To help you become more involved in government and politics—by giving you hints about how to find internships while you are in college and jobs after graduation.

LEARNING SKILLS

Some parts of this guide are geared toward acquainting you with a few of the basic study skills needed to do well in an American government course (and other courses as well). This introduction and several chapters discuss topics such as student survival skills, how to read a textbook, outlining the text, and reading charts and graphs.

REINFORCING YOUR READING

Some parts of the study guide are intended to help you read *The Challenge of Democracy*, Brief Edition, more effectively. Each chapter of the study guide contains a set of learning objectives, listing things you should be able to do after studying the chapter. Next, you'll find a summary isolating the main themes of the overall text as they relate to the content of the chapter. There are also overviews of each chapter and sample exam questions, both multiple-choice and essay.

FINDING OUT MORE

The remaining sections, "Research and Resources," "Using Your Knowledge," and "Getting Involved," take you beyond the text itself. Each "Research and Resources" section tells you about reference materials you may not have encountered before. Some of these sections will be helpful if you are writing a paper on a topic in American government. Others will be helpful to political science majors who go on to do additional course work calling for more advanced research.

Some parts may be useful to students in other fields of study. The "Research and Resources" sections of Chapters 8 through 11, for example, explain how to find government documents. The U.S. government publishes enormous amounts of information on almost every topic under the sun. Although they are usually overlooked, government documents can be an excellent source of material for term papers in other fields. Finally, "Research and Resources" tells you how to find material useful to a citizen who wants to be well informed. In Chapter 4, for example, you'll learn something about the ideological orientation of several journals of opinion. In Chapter 12, you'll learn how to use the Freedom of Information Act to obtain information from the government.

The "Research and Resources" sections contain references to old and new technologies. We've continued to include plenty of old-fashioned paper sources to be found in your library. We also recognize that the phenomenal growth of the Internet has put vast quantities of material on government and politics only a few keystrokes away from most college students. But the Internet also introduces its own set of challenges. On one level, the Internet appears pretty egalitarian—anyone with a computer, a modem, and a few dollars a month can surf the Internet and start creating his or her own Web pages. If you have spent any time at all on the Internet, you know that its great treasures are surrounded by plenty of flotsam and jetsam! How do you identify high-quality material on the Internet? The sites listed at the end of each chapter in the text and in this study guide give you good starting points for answering that question. When you use the Internet as a research tool, train yourself to be a critical thinker. Ask yourself, who is responsible for putting the information out there? You should also ask yourself what biases they have and what their purpose is for posting the page. Is the page intended to inform or persuade? Is there any indication of the author's qualifications or reliability? Are there references pointing to the sources of the author's information, or might the page be simply a collection of opinions, assertions, claims, and speculations?

When you use the material from the Internet, it is important to document your sources just as carefully as if you had drawn ideas from printed sources like books. Because the Internet is still relatively new, scholars have not yet agreed upon a single method for citing Internet sources. You can find several excellent samples of citation styles on-line at <http://www.columbia.edu/cu/cup/cgos/idx_basic.html>. At a minimum, however, your citation should include (1) the author's name, (2) the title of the Web page, (3) the URL (Web address, usually starting with http://), and (4) the date accessed. If there is no author indicated on the Web page, it might be appropriate to substitute the name of the organization sponsoring the page, if it appears on an organizational Web site.

As you read the chapters in the text, ask yourself what kind of democracy might the Internet produce—pluralist or majoritarian? Does the Internet promote or detract from freedom, order, and equality? Think about these matters as you proceed through the course.

The "Research and Resources" sections are followed by exercises titled "Using Your Knowledge." These exercises usually include one or more questions designed to give you some practice using the resources just introduced to you. The questions vary considerably in the amount of time and effort needed to answer them. Some may be completed in half an hour or less. Others could quite easily become term paper topics.

STUDENT SURVIVAL SKILLS

Most likely, the American government course you are taking will be only one of four, five, or even six courses you expect to complete this term. That means you face the task of reading and digesting large quantities of information and learning new skills in several different areas. Sometimes, the mountain of material to be learned can seem much too formidable. How can you make the task more manageable? How will you ever survive the semester? This study guide will help you tackle this problem in your American government course. Some of the hints contained here may also help you in other classes.

Studying is a somewhat idiosyncratic process. We all develop our own individual styles, so what works well for one person does not always work well for another. Nonetheless, a few generally acknowledged practices usually improve student performance. The hints that follow offer nothing very brilliant or profound, but by and large, if you follow them, you will be on the road to success in the course.

First, go to class. Go every day. Researchers looking into the relationships among college grades, class attendance, and student study habits report class attendance to be the best predictor of student grades, not time spent studying. Students who go to class regularly obtain better grades than students who do not go to class. In class, teachers usually tell students what they think is important, and the things teachers think are important tend to crop up again—on tests and exams.

Learn good note-taking skills to make the most of your time in class. Good note takers do not write down every word; they listen carefully and think about what the lecturer is saying. As you listen to a lecture, try to figure out its thesis or central point. Try to pick out the examples of arguments used as evidence to support these points or to illustrate them. Write down (or, when possible, ask) any questions you have about lecture material. Read over your lecture notes soon after class and fill in the blanks while your memory is fresh. Be sure to pursue with your instructor any unresolved questions you have.

Get into the habit of reading the assignment before going to the lecture. If you have read the relevant chapter in *The Challenge of Democracy,* Brief Edition, before attending the lecture, you should be able to understand the lecture more easily, and you will be more likely to have encountered key vocabulary words that may be used in the lecture. You will have a general sense of the problems or issues likely to be discussed in the lecture, and you will be able to question and evaluate both the text and the lecture. If your instructor teaches in an interactive style or grades on participation, reading before class is not only helpful, it is crucial.

Finally, try to plan your time. Keep a calendar. Mark on it all the tests and paper due dates for your classes. Write in your social commitments and other activities. Develop a long-range plan for study and research by scheduling blocks of time in which to do the work required of you. Probably no human being alive ever sticks completely to such a plan, and no doubt you will cheat a little every now and then. But if a great opportunity for a party or a weekend trip comes up, try to figure out exactly how you will rearrange (not eliminate) your study time to accommodate a change in your long-range plan.

Develop a daily schedule. Plan specific hours for study, classes, recreation, and rest. Do not let yourself fall into the habit of studying only when there is nothing else to do! When you find yourself subtracting from planned study time, start looking for specific opportunities to make up the lost hours.

HOW TO READ A TEXTBOOK, OR "MEETING *THE CHALLENGE OF DEMOCRACY"*

One reason why class attendance is a better predictor of student performance than time spent studying is that students vary enormously in their ability to use study time effectively. This study guide will help you use your time to the best effect so that you can meet and master *The Challenge of Democracy.* However, the study guide is no substitute for the text. It can help you focus your reading of the text, but it cannot eliminate the need to read the text closely.

When you first sit down to read *The Challenge of Democracy,* Brief Edition, treat it the way you would (or should) treat any new textbook. On your first approach to the text, try to look at the entire forest, not just the trees—that is, look at the book as a whole, not as a series of separate daily assignments to be performed over a fifteen- or sixteen-week period. Remember that the authors (by the way, what are their names? make a note of them!) have a sense of American government and politics as a whole. Read the preface—what did the authors have in mind when they wrote the book? How do they explain the approach they take in the book? Look at the contents. How is the book organized? What does each part do? What are the chapters in each part? How do the parts fit together? Look at the end of the book. Are there appendixes? Is there a glossary? An index? Thumb through the book. Are there any special sections of special illustrations?

Now you are ready to start work on Chapter 1. But before you begin, pick up this study guide and open it to Chapter 1. Read the section titled "Learning Objectives." Next, preview the text chapter itself; that is, look at its organization. Page through the chapter and note the headings that appear in the text. Look at the photos and illustrations. Read the list of key terms. Next, read the chapter introduction carefully. What is the purpose of the opening vignette? What issues does it raise? What are the main questions posed by the chapter?

Read the chapter carefully, with a pen, pencil, or highlighter in hand. Mark the key sentences in each section. Use some discrimination. Try to select the sentences or phrases in each section that best summarize the major point of the section. Do not highlight everything. Do not be lulled into thinking that because you have colored an entire page yellow, pink, blue, or green that you know and understand the material you have beautified. Instead, next to a sentence you have underlined, make a note in the margin to remind you why you underlined it. Next to the spot where a key term is introduced and defined, you might want to add, for example, *def*. You might want to draw lines in the margins next to examples that illustrate points. Mark these places as examples. You should also use the margins to add your reactions to the material: Does it surprise you? Do you have difficulty understanding it? Do you have difficulty accepting or believing it? What seems to cause the trouble? Do you find contradictions? Write down your questions and problems.

When you finish the chapter, look closely at the chapter summary. Did the author answer the questions posed at the outset? How? Now look closely at the list of key terms. Be sure you can explain each one. Next, turn again to the learning objectives in this study guide. See if you can do each of the things described. Read through the theme summary that precedes the chapter overview.

Now you should be ready to test yourself. Answer the multiple-choice questions. (Do this on a separate piece of paper so you can retest yourself at exam time.) Read the essay questions, and outline the key points you would include in responding to them.

After your instructor has lectured on the material, review the chapter one more time. Look at the outline again, and reread the introduction and the summary. Then review the theme summary and chapter overview in the study guide. Make sure that you still remember the key concepts, and go through the learning objectives one more time. Now read the "Research and Resources" section, and try one or more of the "Using Your Knowledge" exercises.

In addition to these steps (which take time), you may also want to consider outlining the chapter. This exercise helps you focus your attention and forces you to come to grips with the organization of each chapter and the hierarchical relationships among the points made. For more suggestions and a sample outline of Chapter 1 of the text, see Chapter 1 of this study guide.

At the end of the course, when you start thinking about the final exam, repeat the process you used when you started the course. Look over the textbook as a whole. Ask how its main themes were carried through. What were the major ideas developed in the text? How do the specific chapters help to explore or develop those ideas?

BEYOND *THE CHALLENGE OF DEMOCRACY*

Most teachers of American government try to explain systems, processes, values, institutions, and behavior in American politics and government. Few think of themselves as "current events" teachers. Yet, the principles of American government come alive daily—on network newscasts and in daily newspapers. To get the most out of the course, you should try to read a newspaper such as the *New York Times*, *Washington Post*, or *Christian Science Monitor* regularly. You might also consider keeping abreast of current political matters by subscribing to a weekly newsmagazine such as *Time* or *Newsweek*. Get into the habit of watching a network news broadcast or the *Newshour* on PBS. (Many of these resources now have Web sites, with addresses given elsewhere in this study guide or in your text.)

As your knowledge of the principles of American government increases, you will find it easier and easier to comprehend and evaluate information from all these sources.

Finally, there is one absolutely critical source for people studying American government: the *CQ Weekly*. This publication is a very clearly written, concise summary of American politics, focusing heavily on Congress but not neglecting the courts, the president, or other areas such as politics and elections. Check this well-indexed publication each week to find out the latest about events in Washington.

This study guide tries to move you beyond *The Challenge of Democracy* in other ways as well. Several chapters include sections entitled "Getting Involved." These sections provide some general information about jobs or internships available in American politics and government, either with the government itself or with political parties or groups trying to influence or study the governmental process. Although it was not possible to list every possible internship opportunity or to go into great detail about the job-seeking process, you should get some idea of the range of opportunities available. Some of the internships are paid, full-time positions. Far more of them are unpaid. Some of the internships are offered in the summer, others during the academic year, and still others for short periods year-round. Many of the unpaid internships offer experience for which your college or university may give academic credit. Some of the internships are part time, so even if you need to earn money for school, you might be able to combine one of these with a job. Many excellent sources are available for learning more about internship and employment opportunities. For starters, check these two publications: *Careers and the Study of Political Science: A Guide for Undergraduates* and *Storming Washington: An Intern's Guide*. They can be ordered from the American Political Science Association, 1527 New Hampshire Ave. NW, Washington, DC 20036.

CHAPTER 1

Dilemmas of Democracy

LEARNING OBJECTIVES

After reading this chapter you should be able to

- Define the key terms identified in the chapter margins.

- Discuss the increasing impact of globalization on American politics.

- Give practical examples of ways that the values of freedom, order, and equality may conflict.

- Provide a conceptual framework for analyzing government.

- Discuss the three major purposes of government.

- Explain the two dilemmas of government.

- Sketch a continuum of ideological stances on the scope of government, ranging from totalitarianism to anarchism.

- Construct a two-dimensional, fourfold classification of American political ideologies, using the values of freedom, order, and equality.

- Distinguish between liberals and conservatives with regard to their attitudes about the scope and purpose of government.

- List the four principles of procedural democracy.

- Outline the central principles of the substantive view of democracy.

- Point out the differences between the procedural and the substantive views of democracy and indicate the key problems with each.

- Explain why representative democracy has replaced participatory democracy in the modern world.

- Compare and contrast the assumptions and mechanisms of the majoritarian, pluralist, and elite models.

- Discuss the pressures faced by newly democratizing states.

- Make a preliminary attempt to identify the strengths and weaknesses of the majoritarian, pluralist, and elite models as they apply to the American system.

DILEMMAS OF DEMOCRACY AND THE CHALLENGE OF DEMOCRACY

This chapter begins with a discussion of the war in Iraq and introduces the concept of globalization. The increasing interdependence of citizens and nations across the world affects American politics in a number of ways that will be explored in this text. The discussion of the terrorist attacks also raises several profound questions about values that often stand in tension with each other. The chapter then explores the meaning of three of the text's five major themes: freedom, order, and equality. These values are important in the American political system. They often come into conflict with one another, however, and thus pose a dilemma for people forced to choose among competing values. For example, the conflict in Iraq pits the value of order (in the form of personal and national security) against that of freedom. The chapter outlines two major conflicts over the purpose and scope of government raised by these competing values, namely, the conflict between freedom and order (also called the *original dilemma*) and the conflict between freedom and equality (referred to as the *modern dilemma*).

The chapter then introduces another basic theme of the text—namely, the conflict between the majoritarian and pluralist models of democracy. To illustrate this conflict, we give the example of the politics of gun control, focusing on the seesawing battle over gun control in the wake of the tragic murders at Columbine High School. This conflict pitted the National Rifle Association (NRA), a well-organized interest group, against the overwhelming majority of Americans, who support background checks on individuals purchasing weapons at gun shows. Though the public supported such checks, legislation mandating them stalled in Congress. The case raised important questions about the nature of democracy in America. Isn't democracy supposed to follow the will of the majority? Under a majoritarian model, the House of Representatives should have responded to public opinion and enacted the legislation. But the history of the gun control issue shows how an extremely well-organized and well-financed lobby can convince Congress to go against public opinion—an example of the pluralist model of democracy in action.

The remainder of the text contains many examples of the conflict among the values of freedom, order, and equality. In addition, political institutions and processes are analyzed to show how well they fit the majoritarian or pluralist model.

CHAPTER OVERVIEW

The Challenge of Democracy argues that good government involves tough choices. The authors encourage you to think about what government does and also about what it should and should not do. The text emphasizes the dilemmas that confront governments when they must choose between conflicting values.

The Purposes of Government

Government is the legitimate use of force to control human behavior. Throughout history, government has served three major purposes: (1) maintaining order, including preserving life and protecting property; (2) providing public goods; and (3) promoting equality. Maintaining order, the first purpose, is the oldest and least-contended purpose of government. Most would agree with Thomas Hobbes that the security of civil society is preferable to life in a warlike state of nature. But the question of whether maintaining order requires the government to protect private property finds philosophers such as John Locke and Karl Marx at odds.

The second purpose—providing public goods—leads to questions of just what goods the government ought to provide. Over the years, the scope of American government has expanded considerably as the government has assumed greater responsibility for providing an array of social benefits. The third purpose of government—promoting equality—is the newest and probably the most controversial purpose of government today. It raises issues about the extent of the government's role in redistributing wealth, regulating social behavior, and providing for opportunity.

A Conceptual Framework for Analyzing Government

People often have difficulty understanding American government because they lack a framework to help them organize the facts of politics. The framework supplied in this text distinguishes between the values citizens pursue through government and the *institutional models* that guide them in their efforts to govern themselves democratically. The framework presented here uses five major concepts. Three of these concepts—freedom, order, and equality—represent *what* democratic governments try to do. The two remaining concepts concern *how* democratic governments do what they do; governments may behave according to pluralistic or majoritarian models.

The Concepts of Freedom, Order, and Equality. *Freedom,* as used in this text, is synonymous with *liberty*—that is, the freedom to speak, worship, and so forth. In a narrow sense, *order* consists of preserving life and protecting property, but it may also refer to social order, which prescribes the accepted way of doing things. *Equality* is used to mean several different things: *political equality,* or equality of influence in the political process; *social equality,* or equality in wealth, education, and social status; *equality of opportunity,* or equality in chances for success; and *equality of outcome,* or equality for people in the end. The last concept is connected with the idea of entitlements and requires much more government intervention to sustain than do either political equality or equality of opportunity.

Two Dilemmas of Government. Two major dilemmas confront the government today. The first, or the "original dilemma," involves tradeoffs between freedom and order. How much freedom are people willing to give up to achieve complete safety? How much insecurity are we willing to tolerate to preserve our personal freedom? The second, or the "modern dilemma," deals with the balance between freedom and equality. Should government act to promote equal access for women and blacks to well-paying jobs, even though this restricts the freedom of their employers?

Ideology and Government. Political ideologies provide their adherents with consistent, organized beliefs about government. Each ideology provides a different answer to questions about the scope of government, that is, how far government should go in maintaining order, providing public goods, and promoting equality.

Totalitarians would place everything under governmental control. *Socialists* would control basic industries but might leave room for some private ownership of productive capacities and for the practice of civil liberties. *Capitalists* favor private ownership of the means of production and no government interference with business. *Libertarians* oppose government action except where absolutely necessary to protect life and property. *Anarchists* oppose all government.

Practical politics in the United States tends to be fought out in the middle ground of this continuum—a place inhabited by conservatives and liberals who differ on both the scope and the purpose of government action. In the past, liberals and conservatives have been distinguished by their attitudes toward the scope of government. Today, this approach is not quite adequate; ideological divisions among Americans involve not only disagreements over the scope of government but also disagreements about the purposes of government, that is, the degree to which the government should promote freedom, order, and equality.

A Two-Dimensional Classification of Ideologies. Liberals and conservatives differ on both of the major value conflicts described in this chapter. By using a two-dimensional classification system that depicts freedom and order on one axis and freedom and equality on the other, it is possible to obtain a more accurate picture of the differences between liberals and conservatives. This scheme yields a fourfold classification of American political ideologies. Under it, those who prefer order to freedom and freedom to equality are *conservatives*. Those who prefer equality to freedom and freedom to order are *liberals*. Those who prefer freedom above the other values are *libertarians*. Those who would give up freedom for either equality or order are called *communitarians*.

The American Governmental Process: Majoritarian or Pluralist?

The authors use a House of Representatives vote on the repeal of an assault weapons ban to redirect our attention from the study of the values government should pursue to an examination of *how* government should decide what to do and whether its decision-making process is democratic.

The Theory of Democratic Government. Historically, rule by the people—democracy—was greeted with scorn; in the modern world, however, most governments try to style themselves as democratic.

This chapter provides methods for deciding on the validity of their claims. It defines democracy and tries to show what kind of a democracy the United States is.

The authors present two different theories of democracy. The first, a procedural theory, emphasizes how decisions are made. It relies on four main principles: universal participation, political equality, majority rule, and responsiveness of representatives to the electorate. Under the requirements of the procedural theory, there need be no protections for minorities. The second theory, a substantive one, pays more attention to the content of what government does. Substantive theorists generally expect the government to protect the basic civil rights and liberties of all, including minorities; some substantive theorists go further and expect the government to ensure various social and economic rights. The difficulty with substantive theory is that it is hard to reach agreement on the scope of government involvement in these social and economic matters.

Institutional Models of Democracy. Democracies today are representative democracies rather than participatory democracies. They require institutional mechanisms to translate public opinion into government policies. These institutional mechanisms might be designed to tie governmental policies closely to the will of the *majority,* or they may be structured to allow *groups* of citizens to defend their interests before government.

The classic model of democracy is the *majoritarian model.* It assumes a population of knowledgeable voters who willingly go to the polls to vote on issues and to select candidates whom they have decided, through rational evaluation, will best represent them. The main tools of majoritarian democracy are elections, referenda, and initiatives. (Although public opinion in the United States supports national referenda, referenda and initiatives are available only at the state and local levels.) While proponents of majoritarian democracy point to the stability of public opinion and to Americans' desires to become more involved in politics, critics argue that majoritarian assumptions do not correspond very well to American political reality. For example, in the United States, citizens aren't well informed, and voter turnout is low.

A second model, the *pluralist model,* better reflects the limited knowledge and participation of the real electorate. It envisions democratic politics taking place within an arena of interest groups. This model relies on open access that allows individuals to organize into groups to press their claims on multiple centers of governmental power (Congress, state legislatures, bureaucratic agencies, and so on).

A third model, *elite theory,* which is also discussed in this chapter, is more of an antidemocratic theory. Elite theory maintains that democracy is a sham because power is really in the hands of a small number of individuals who control all governmental decisions and manipulate the political agenda. Yet, in American politics, it seems that, although a small group of people may have a big impact, the groups that are effective change with each issue. This observation undermines the elite theory.

KEY TERMS

globalization

government

national sovereignty

order

communism

public goods

freedom of

freedom from

police power

political equality

social equality

equality of opportunity

equality of outcome

rights

political ideology

totalitarianism

socialism

democratic socialism

capitalism

libertarianism

laissez faire

anarchism

liberals

conservatives

communitarians

democracy

procedural democratic theory

universal participation

majority rule

participatory democracy

representative democracy

responsiveness

substantive democratic theory

minority rights

majoritarian model of democracy

interest group

pluralist model of democracy

elite theory

oligarchy

democratization

OUTLINING THE TEXT CHAPTERS

One good way to learn the material in your text is to outline each chapter after you have read it. This will help you understand how a chapter is organized and how its main points fit together. The act of writing out the outline focuses your attention on the material and also reinforces what you've read.

Outlining styles tend to be idiosyncratic: one person might prepare an outline that uses full sentences or long phrases to help recall the substance of sections of the text; another might prefer to rely on brief phrases or key words. For starters though, you may want to use the chapter's *main headings* and *subheadings* as the skeleton for your outline. Then flesh these out by noting the main points within each subheading, and where you think it is useful, add some notes to indicate how each point is connected to the main heading.

Here is a sample outline of Chapter 1.

CHAPTER ONE—OUTLINE

I. The globalization of American government
    A. Definition of government: the legitimate use of force within territorial boundaries to control human behavior; also, the organization or agency authorized to exercise that force.
    B. National sovereignty stands in tension with international agreements and the growing economic and political interdependence of nations.
II. The purposes of government
    A. Maintain order
        1. Survival
        2. Protecting private property
    B. Provide public goods
        1. Public goods—benefits available to all citizens that are not likely to be produced voluntarily by individuals
        2. Tension between government vs. private business
    C. Promote equality
        1. Economic: redistributing wealth
        2. Social: regulate social behavior
        3. Tension between equality and freedom
III. A conceptual framework for analyzing government
    A. Definition of concept: a generalized idea of a class of items or thoughts under a common classification or label
    B. Five concepts used in this text
        1. What government tries to do (values)
            a. freedom
            b. order
            c. equality
        2. How governments do it (models)
            a. pluralist
            b. majoritarian
IV. The concepts of freedom, order, and equality
    A. Freedom
        1. Freedom of: liberty
        2. Freedom from: immunity, or, as used in this text, equality
    B. Order
        1. Preserving life
        2. Protecting property
        3. Maintaining social order

         4.   Use of police power

   C.   Equality

         1.   Political equality

                a.   one person, one vote

                b.   ability to influence political decisions through wealth or status

         2.   Social equality

                a.   equality of opportunity: each person has the same chance to succeed in life

                b.   equality of outcome

                        (1).   government redistributes wealth to ensure that economic equality and social equality are achieved

                        (2).   governmental rights as entitlements

V.   Two dilemmas of government

   A.   The original dilemma: freedom vs. order

   B.   The modern dilemma: freedom vs. equality

VI.   Ideology and government

   A.   Definition of political ideology: a consistent set of values and beliefs about the proper purpose and scope of government

   B.   Continuum of ideologies based on beliefs about governmental scope

         1.   Totalitarianism: controls all aspects of behavior in all sectors of society

         2.   Socialism

                a.   from Marxist theory

                b.   state has broad scope of authority in the economic life of the nation

                c.   communism vs. democratic socialism

         3.   Capitalism

                a.   private business operating without government regulations

                b.   American capitalism: some regulation of business and direction of overall economy

         4.   Libertarianism

                a.   opposed to all government action except what is necessary to protect life and property

                b.   opposed to government intervention in the economy

         5.   Anarchism: opposed to all government

   C.   Liberals and conservatives

         1.   Liberals

                a.   favor broad scope of government in providing public goods

                b.   yet reject censorship, regulation of abortion

         2.   Conservatives

                a.   oppose government role as activist in economy

                b.   favor small government

                c.   yet favor government regulation of social behavior

         3.   Need to look at both scope and purpose of government action

   D.   Liberals vs. conservatives: the new differences

         1.   Conservatives

                a.   scope of government: narrow

                b.   purpose of government: maintain social order

                        (1).   coercive power of state may be used to force citizens to be orderly

                        (2).   preserve traditional patterns of social relations

         2.   Liberals

                a.   scope of government: broad

                b.   purpose of government: promote equality (coercive power of state may be used)

   E.   Two-dimensional classification of ideologies

    1.   Dimensions
        a.   freedom—order
        b.   freedom—equality
    2.   Four ideological types
        a.   libertarians
            (1). value freedom more than order
            (2). value freedom more than equality
        b.   liberals
            (1). value freedom more than order
            (2). value equality more than freedom
        c.   conservatives
            (1). value freedom more than equality
            (2). value order more than freedom
        d.   communitarians
            (1). value equality more than freedom
            (2). value order more than freedom

VII. American governmental process: majoritarian or pluralist?
    A.   In failing to pass a requirement for background checks at gun shows, the House of Representatives supported a small constituency (NRA, gun owners, etc.) rather than the majority of Americans who favor gun control.
    B.   Is the United States democratic?
    C.   The theory of democratic government
        1.   Americans believe in democracy ("rule by the people")
            a.   *Which* people?
            b.   *How* do the people govern?
        2.   Procedural view of democracy focuses on how decisions are made
            a.   universal participation: everyone participates
            b.   political equality: all votes count equally
            c.   majority rule: majority decides for all
            d.   responsiveness: elected officials should be responsive to public opinion
        3.   Direct vs. indirect democracy
            a.   direct (participatory democracy): all members meet and decide
            b.   indirect (representative democracy): elected officials represent citizens
        4.   Substantive view of democracy
            a.   government practices must be in accordance with certain principles
            b.   substantive theorists generally agree on inclusion of civil liberties and civil rights
            c.   substantive theorists disagree on inclusion of social and economic rights
                (1). conservative: narrow view
                (2). liberal: broad government responsibility
        5.   Procedural democracy vs. substantive democracy
            a.   substantive doesn't provide clear criteria for democratic government
            b.   procedural can promote policies that ignore minority rights
    D.   Institutional models of democracy
        1.   Majoritarian model
            a.   interprets "government by the people" as government by the majority of the people
            b.   mechanisms
                (1). popular election of officials
                (2). referendum
                (3). initiative
            c.   no referenda or initiatives at the federal level in the United States

    2.   Pluralist model
        a.   pluralism: society consists of many groups with shared interests
        b.   interest group: organized group that seeks to influence public policy
        c.   interprets "government by the people" as government by people operating through competing interest groups
        d.   Constitution approaches pluralist ideal by dividing authority among many branches and levels of government
    3.   Majoritarian model vs. pluralist model
        a.   majoritarian
            (1). active, knowledgeable electorate
            (2). electoral mechanisms for majority decisions
            (3). centralized government
    4.   An undemocratic model: elite theory
        a.   views United States as an oligarchy, not a democracy
            (1). small, powerful minority makes most important decisions
            (2). minority is stable and identifiable
        b.   studies don't generally support elite theory
    5.   Elite theory vs. pluralist theory
        a.   key difference: durability of the ruling elites
        b.   pluralist theory
            (1). many minorities vie with one another in each policy area
            (2). no identifiable elite wins constantly
            (3). public benefits from government structures that facilitate group access
            (4). unorganized elements not equally represented
VIII. Democracy and globalization
    A.   Most countries are neither majoritarian nor pluralist, but authoritarian.
    B.   U.S. democracy: more pluralist than majoritarian
       1.   United States fits the pluralist model better than the majoritarian
       2.   Pluralist democracy is imperfect: favors well-organized, often wealthier elements

RESEARCH AND RESOURCES

This chapter introduces three of the key concepts used to build the analytical framework of the text. Freedom, order, and equality are such important concepts and are so critical to the approach of *The Challenge of Democracy* that you might wish to learn more about these ideas. One way to do that is to consult an encyclopedia or dictionary, such as the *Encyclopedia Britannica* or *Webster's New World Dictionary*. (Access to *Britannica* is available as a paid service on-line. For a free trial, try <http://www.eb.com/>.) In these works, you will find a general treatment of the terms. A general encyclopedic discussion may include some material of interest to social scientists, but it may also include material more interesting to people in other fields. (For example, philosophers might be more interested in the question of free will versus determinism, a question often included in general discussions of freedom.) These general reference works, while useful, may not provide quite the depth you want, however. You may find it helpful to turn to a more specialized work tailored to providing information about subjects as they apply to social or political science.

The following are some useful specialized dictionaries and encyclopedias:

Calhoun, Craig, ed. *Dictionary of the Social Sciences.* New York: Oxford University Press, 2000.

Kuper, Adam, and Jessica Kuper, eds. *The Social Science Encyclopedia,* 2d ed. New York: Routledge, 1996.

Shafritz, Jay M. *The HarperCollins Dictionary of American Government and Politics*. New York: HarperCollins, 1992.

The above works are not updated very frequently, and they are geared to provide an introduction to or overview of a subject. If you need in-depth information, you will probably want to start by looking for books on your subject or specialized journals with the most recent research. At the back of your textbook, you can find a list of suggested readings for each chapter, and the electronic information superhighway now makes it possible for many students to look beyond the confines of their own campus and visit the catalogs of many of the finest libraries in the world using the Internet. When you discover books on your topic that are not in your library, check with your librarian to see if you can arrange for an interlibrary loan. Many colleges and libraries subscribe to political science journals in electronic format as well as traditional paper. Ask your librarian whether you have access to journal articles on the World Wide Web through JSTOR, Academic Search Elite, or a similar service.

USING YOUR KNOWLEDGE

1. Become familiar with specialized encyclopedias and dictionaries. Look up the terms *equality, freedom, democracy, ideology,* and *pluralism* in works such as those cited above. Compare the material covered in the different sources. Are all these terms included in every work?

2. At the end of Chapter 1, there is a list of internet exercises. Visit the Freedom House site discussed in the first exercise and explore the civil rights ratings of countries that you think of as allies to the United States. After exploring the Web site a bit, does it seem that Freedom House itself represents a liberal, conservative, libertarian, or communitarian viewpoint? Why?

SAMPLE EXAM QUESTIONS

Multiple-Choice Questions

(Answers to multiple-choice questions are at the end of the chapter)

1. "The legitimate use of force to control human behavior within territorial boundaries" is a definition of
    a. politics.
    b. government.
    c. democracy.
    d. totalitarianism.
2. A principle that states that each citizen has one and only one vote is a principle of
    a. political equality.
    b. social equality.
    c. equality of opportunity.
    d. equality of outcome.
3. According to Thomas Hobbes, the main purpose of government is to
    a. distribute ownership of property in an equitable manner.
    b. protect private property.
    c. protect the physical security of citizens.
    d. increase the glory of the Leviathan-like ruler.

4. The political philosopher who first argued that the main purpose of government is to protect the "life, liberty, and property of its citizens" was

    a.   Karl Marx.
    b.   John Locke.
    c.   Thomas Jefferson.
    d.   Thomas Hobbes.

5. The modern dilemma of government can be seen in

    a.   using the smallpox vaccine to protect the military against bioterror attacks.
    b.   a city's effort to prosecute store owners for selling CDs with obscene lyrics.
    c.   the implementation of school busing to achieve racial balance.
    d.   All of the above.

6. Totalitarian states

    a.   are all communist.
    b.   try to regulate all aspects of individual behavior.
    c.   limit the scope of government to produce a perfect society.
    d.   always outlaw private ownership of the means of production.

7. The political ideology that rejects all government action *except* that which is necessary to protect life and property is called

    a.   liberalism.
    b.   libertarianism.
    c.   capitalism.
    d.   anarchism.

8. The original dilemma of government pits

    a.   democracy against communism.
    b.   order against freedom.
    c.   equality against freedom.
    d.   equality against order.

9. The modern dilemma of government involves the clash between

    a.   democracy and communism.
    b.   equality and majoritarian rule.
    c.   equality and freedom.
    d.   equality and order.

10. The term *freedom,* as used in the text, is synonymous with

    a.   equality.
    b.   liberty.
    c.   equality of outcome.
    d.   equality of opportunity.

11. A person who values order and equality more than freedom would be called a(n)

    a.   anarchist.
    b.   libertarian.
    c.   communitarian.
    d.   conservative.

12. All of the following are true *except* that

    a.   libertarians value freedom above equality.
    b.   liberals value equality more than order.
    c.   conservatives value freedom more than equality.
    d.   communitarians value freedom more than order.

13. All governments require that citizens

    a.   treat one another equally and fairly.
    b.   serve in the military in some capacity.
    c.   give up some freedom in the process of being governed.
    d.   pledge allegiance to their flag.

14. Typically, it is safe to assume that freedom and equality

    a.   go hand in hand.
    b.   are generally unrelated to each other in most political spheres.
    c.   are valued equally by all major ideologies.
    d.   conflict when governments enact policies to promote social equality.

15. A law prohibiting flag burning would

    a.   be favored by anarchists.
    b.   raise the original dilemma of government.
    c.   pit freedom against equality.
    d.   pit order against equality.

16. Socialism differs from communism as it was practiced in the Soviet Union and Eastern European countries because socialism

    a.   does not advocate government ownership and control of basic industries.
    b.   does not favor a strong government role in regulating private industry and directing the economy.
    c.   has no connection to Marxist theory.
    d.   does not necessarily seek to control both political and social life through a dominant party organization.

17. Libertarians would be most likely to support

    a.   a government-sponsored Just Say No program to combat drug use.
    b.   a Mothers Against Drunk Driving campaign to raise the drinking age.
    c.   deregulation of the airlines.
    d.   a constitutional amendment to prohibit flag burning.

18. An election that allows voters to make a choice on a policy issue is called a(n)

    a.   referendum.
    b.   initiative.
    c.   recall.
    d.   public opinion poll.

19. The procedural theory of democracy upholds all of the following principles *except*

    a.   political equality.
    b.   majority rule.
    c.   universal participation.
    d.   protection of minorities.

20. The principle of responsiveness

    a.   protects minority rights.
    b.   is unnecessary in representative democracy.
    c.   disallows prayer in public schools.
    d.   requires elected officials to do what the people want.

21. Compared to citizens of most other industrialized nations, Americans tend to be more religious. A move to require prayer in public schools would probably be consistent with

    a.   both substantive and procedural democracy.
    b.   substantive democracy but not procedural democracy.
    c.   procedural democracy but not substantive democracy.
    d.   neither procedural nor substantive democracy.

22. The majoritarian model of democratic government
    a.   offers protection for minority rights.
    b.   relies on a relatively passive citizenry.
    c.   expects citizens to have a high degree of knowledge.
    d.   fits well with the behavior of voters in America.

23. The form of democracy suitable to small societies where people rule themselves is called
    a.   representative democracy.
    b.   indirect democracy.
    c.   participatory democracy.
    d.   procedural democracy.

24. The pluralist theory of democracy
    a.   is basically the same as majoritarian theory in its assumptions about citizens.
    b.   sees democracy operating through the activities of groups.
    c.   rejects decentralization as undemocratic.
    d.   works better in unitary rather than federal systems.

25. Elite theory differs from pluralist theory by defining government conflict in terms of
    a.   many minorities thwarting the majority.
    b.   one durable minority ruling the majority.
    c.   interchangeable minorities and special interests dominating specific policy areas.
    d.   substantive rather than procedural democracy.

26. A model of government that places a high value on participation by people organized in groups is
    a.   elitism.
    b.   substantive democracy.
    c.   pluralism.
    d.   majoritarianism.

27. According to the text, American democracy is best described as
    a.   elitist.
    b.   pluralist.
    c.   majoritarian.
    d.   substantive.

28. In the United States, initiatives and referenda are held at
    a.   the national level only.
    b.   the local level only.
    c.   the national, state, and local levels.
    d.   the state and local levels only.

29. The gun lobby's success in defeating gun control legislation supported by the majority of the electorate is an example of
    a.   pluralist democracy.
    b.   elite theory.
    c.   autocracy.
    d.   majoritarian democracy.

30. Universal participation, political equality, and majority rule are principles that
    a.   define democracy in procedural democratic theory.
    b.   define democracy in substantive democratic theory.
    c.   conflict with one another and are impossible to achieve together in the same system.
    d.   were incorporated into the U.S. Constitution from the beginning.

Essay Questions

1. In *Lawrence and Garner* v. *Texas*, the Supreme Court held that states may not outlaw homosexual practices between consenting adults. Given their respective value systems, how might typical individuals in each of the four ideological categories described in this chapter react to this decision? Explain your conclusions.

2. Why is it important to consider both the scope and the purpose of government action when one classifies ideologies?

3. Explain the key differences between liberals and conservatives in modern U.S. politics.

4. According to the text, the newest major purpose of government is to promote equality. Explain the various meanings of the term *equality*. What aspects of this new purpose of government are controversial in America? Why?

5. Explain how the principles of procedural democracy may threaten liberty.

6. Why do substantive democratic theories create controversy?

7. Describe the majoritarian model of democracy. How well does it fit U.S. political practice?

8. Describe the pluralist model of democracy. How does it differ from elite theory? Which model more accurately fits the U.S. government?

ANSWERS TO MULTIPLE-CHOICE QUESTIONS

1. b
2. a
3. c
4. b
5. c
6. b
7. b
8. b
9. c
10. b
11. c
12. d
13. c
14. d
15. b
16. d
17. c
18. a
19. d
20. d
21. c
22. c
23. c
24. b
25. b
26. c
27. b
28. d
29. a
30. a

CHAPTER 2

The Constitution

LEARNING OBJECTIVES

After reading this chapter you should be able to

- Define the key terms identified in the chapter margins.

- Analyze the conflict between Britain and the colonies.

- Explain how the colonial and revolutionary experiences shaped America's first try at self-government under the Articles of Confederation.

- Account for the failure of the Articles of Confederation.

- Outline the main features of the Virginia and New Jersey Plans and describe the major compromises made by the delegates to the Constitutional Convention.

- Explain the four basic principles underlying the Constitution and show how they reflected Americans' revolutionary values.

- Discuss the way the issue of slavery arose at the Constitutional Convention.

- Summarize the provisions of each article of the Constitution.

- Describe the formal and informal processes of constitutional change.

- Explain how the promise of a bill of rights was used to ensure ratification of the Constitution.

THE CONSTITUTION AND THE CHALLENGE OF DEMOCRACY

The challenge of drafting a constitution acceptable to millions of people with differing interests is no easier in the twenty-first century than it was in the eighteenth. Though the drafting process and the final products looked much different, many of the same challenges that faced the "constitutionalists" of Europe faced the founding fathers of the United States over two centuries earlier. The U.S. Constitution was designed to reconcile order with freedom, a problem this text calls the original dilemma. The founders recognized the need for government to protect life, liberty, and property, but they had just won their freedom from Britain, and they feared that a new, remote national government might threaten the very freedoms it was established to protect. In their first attempt to create a government under the Articles of Confederation, they gave too little power to the national government. As a result, that government was unable to maintain order. In drawing up the Constitution, the founders looked for ways to give adequate power to the national government while still safeguarding freedom. To achieve this end, they designed four principal tools: the separation of powers, checks and balances, republicanism, and federalism.

Although the founders paid a great deal of attention to the conflict between order and freedom, they were not particularly concerned with the tension between freedom and equality—after all, that is a modern dilemma, as the authors of the text point out. The eighteenth-century document accepted slavery and left the qualifications for voting up to the states. As a result, blacks, women, and poor people were all excluded from the political process. Only later did these matters of social and political equality become issues.

With respect to the text's second theme—the conflict between pluralist and majoritarian models—this chapter points out that the constitutional order was designed to be pluralist. The founders were frightened by majority rule and relied on factions' counteracting one another—a mechanism characteristic of pluralism.

CHAPTER OVERVIEW

The U.S. Constitution is very brief, very old, and very durable. Although it was itself the ultimate product of a revolution, it has provided a remarkably stable political framework, able to accommodate America's growth and development from a collection of eighteenth-century agrarian states to a twenty-first-century superpower. The document's own historical roots grew out of three experiences: colonialism, revolution, and the failure of the Articles of Confederation.

The Revolutionary Roots of the Constitution

The colonists in America expected to enjoy the rights of Englishmen. These rights included not being taxed without being represented in the government. The colonists had their own colonial legislature, which legislated for them on domestic matters, but Britain controlled overseas trade and foreign affairs. When Britain decided to tax the colonists to pay administrative (including defense) costs, the colonists viewed the taxation as a violation of their right not to be taxed without having representation. The colonies began to unite in their opposition to British policies, and in 1776, colonial delegates to the Second Continental Congress declared America's independence from Britain. The Declaration of Independence set out the philosophical justification for the break. Following arguments developed by English philosopher John Locke nearly a century earlier, Thomas Jefferson asserted that the colonists had inalienable rights to life, liberty, and the pursuit of happiness; that people created governments to protect those rights; and that when a government threatened those rights, the people had the right to alter or abolish it. The declaration then listed a long series of charges against the British king to show how he had violated the colonists' rights, thus justifying their revolution.

From Revolution to Confederation

The Declaration of Independence and the Revolutionary War established that the American colonies would not be governed by England, but they did not determine how the new nation would be governed. In their first effort to structure a system of government, the newly independent Americans established a republic under the Articles of Confederation. This system created a loose confederation that protected the sovereignty of the individual states. The Articles had several major failings: the central government had no power to tax or to regulate interstate or foreign commerce; no real executive was appointed to direct the government; and any amendment to the Articles required unanimous consent of the state legislatures. These flaws crippled the new government. Events such as Shays's Rebellion soon underscored the need for a new form of government better equipped to maintain order.

From Confederation to Constitution

The delegates charged with "revising" the Articles quickly agreed that more than minor changes were required. They debated the Virginia Plan, which included among its provisions a strong central government with three branches (legislative, executive, and judicial); a two-chamber legislature, which could negate state laws (with representation in proportion to taxes paid or in proportion to the free population); and an executive selected by the legislature and limited to one term. Much of the Virginia Plan was adopted but only after challenges and amendments. In particular, small states believed that the Virginia Plan did not represent their interests. One small-state challenge came in the form of the New Jersey Plan, which gave less power to the central government and proposed a one-chamber legislature in which states would have equal representation.

To solve the conflict between the big and small states over representation, the delegates fashioned the Great (or "Connecticut") Compromise. Under this arrangement, each state would have equal representation in the Senate and representation according to its population in the House of Representatives. Revenue bills would have to originate in the House.

Additional compromises resulted in a one-person executive who would serve a four-year term and be eligible for reelection. This executive (the president) would be selected by an electoral college, in which states would have the same number of votes as they have in the two chambers of Congress combined.

The Final Product

The Constitution begins with a preamble that creates a people, explains the reasons for the Constitution, articulates the goals of the government, and fashions that government. The Constitution is based on four major principles: republicanism, in which power resides in the people and is exercised by their representatives; federalism, which divides power between the national and state governments; separation of powers, which gives different powers to each branch of government and prevents any one person or group from monopolizing power; and checks and balances, which gives each branch some power to limit the actions of the other branches. The first of the seven articles of the Constitution establishes a bicameral (two-chambered) legislature endowed with eighteen enumerated powers, including the powers to tax and spend and to regulate interstate commerce. The "elastic clause" (Article I, Section 8) gives Congress the powers necessary to effect its enumerated powers.

The office of the executive is created in Article II, which describes the qualifications required for the presidency and specifies the process for selecting the president by the electoral college. Article II also lists procedures for removing the president by impeachment and describes the powers of the presidency.

Article III establishes a Supreme Court and specifies the method of appointing and removing judges. Most of the details of the judicial system are left up to Congress.

The remaining articles provide that each state must give full faith and credit to the actions of the other states. They also outline the procedure for admitting new states, establish the procedure for amending the Constitution, and specify that the Constitution is the supreme law of the land.

The men who drafted the Constitution may have been motivated in part by economic issues, but their most important source of motivation was the inability of the national and state governments under the Articles of Confederation to maintain order. Their desire to create a system that would maintain order was so strong that the framers readily compromised to allow the institution of slavery to continue.

Selling the Constitution

The Constitution had to be approved by nine states before it could take effect. The campaigns for and against ratification were intense, and the votes taken in several states were quite close. For people to accept the Constitution, its supporters had to allay fears of governmental threats to freedom. The *Federalist* papers explained and defended the principles of the Constitution. Their authors argued that factions (pluralism), the mechanism of representation, and the application of checks and balances could be used to prevent tyranny. Finally, the promise to add a bill of rights placing certain fundamental rights beyond the bounds of government interference helped win support.

Constitutional Change

The Constitution provides a mechanism for amending it, including two means of proposing amendments (by a convention or by a two-thirds vote in each house of Congress) and two means of ratifying proposed amendments (by three-fourths of the states, either through their legislatures or through state conventions). The amendment process requires extraordinary majorities and makes formal constitutional change fairly difficult.

The Constitution changes in other ways, however. Through judicial interpretation, the courts often give new meaning to constitutional provisions and thus make the Constitution adaptable to a changing world. Changing political practice has also altered the way the Constitution is applied.

An Evaluation of the Constitution

The Constitution was successfully designed to provide the order lacking under the Articles of Confederation, while at the same time protecting the freedom of individuals. However, social and political inequality—the issues that give rise to what is referred to in Chapter 1 as the modern dilemma—were not yet thought of as important goals of government. Only after the Civil War were amendments added that dealt with the issue of inequality.

The Constitution established a republican structure of government, in which the government rests on the consent of the governed. It was not the intent of the framers to create a democracy that rested on majority rule, however. Thus, from the outset, the Constitution was more pluralist than majoritarian.

KEY TERMS

Declaration of Independence

social-contract theory

republic

confederation

Articles of Confederation

Virginia Plan

legislative branch

executive branch

judicial branch

New Jersey Plan

Great Compromise

republicanism

federalism

separation of powers

extraordinary majorities

checks and balances

enumerated powers

necessary and proper clause

implied powers

judicial review

supremacy clause

Bill of Rights

RESEARCH AND RESOURCES

The framers of the Constitution produced a remarkably durable government framework. The system they designed combined strength and flexibility. Over the years, it has evolved and been adapted to fit the needs of the times. As circumstances change, decision makers fashion responses to new situations. The Constitution itself may be silent on a particular matter at issue. Yet, policymakers will often look to the founders for guidance. What exactly did they have in mind when they established a certain constitutional provision? Can a new course of action be justified by showing that it accords with the spirit of the Constitution?

What sources help reveal the intentions of the framers? Generally, good researchers try to rely on primary material—that is, on firsthand accounts, written by the participants themselves, or on official records of the debates—rather than on secondary material such as interpretations offered by analysts not party to the Constitutional Convention. You have already encountered one important primary source of information about the intentions of the founders. The *Federalist* papers, written by "Publius," were in fact coauthored by James Madison, the "Father of the Constitution." (They are available on-line at <http://thomas.loc.gov/home/histdox/fedpapers.html>.) They were written for a polemical purpose— namely, to put the best face possible on the Constitution to sell it to New Yorkers. Still, it has proved a valuable guide to understanding how Madison, at least, expected the Constitution to operate.

Another important primary source of information on the Constitution and the framers' ideas about it is Max Farrand, ed., *The Records of the Federal Convention of 1787* (New Haven, CT: Yale University Press, 1937). In this work, Farrand has compiled, in chronological order, the *Journal* (essentially the minutes of the meetings), as well as the notes made by many of the participants, including James Madison, Alexander Hamilton, Rufus King, James McHenry, George Mason, and others. An extensive index can be found at the end of the fourth volume. Madison's notes have been posted on-line at <http://www.constitution.org/dfc/dfc-0000.htm>.

For an in-depth modern source on the Constitution and its development, you may wish to consult Leonard W. Levy, Kenneth Karst, and Dennis Mahoney, eds., *Encyclopedia of the American Constitution* (New York: Macmillan, 1986).

USING YOUR KNOWLEDGE

1. Using *The Records of the Federal Convention of 1787*, select a delegate to the Convention and imagine yourself in his position. What were his main concerns? What interests did he seem to represent? Why? What role did he play in the Convention? Can you find out anything about his subsequent career?

2. Chapter 2 emphasizes the ways in which the original dilemma of freedom versus order influenced the design of the Constitution. The chapter also mentions the possibility that a new constitutional convention might someday be called. What if such a convention were called and—like the one in 1787—the delegates simply decided to start anew? Speculate on what such a meeting might produce by outlining your own version of a modern constitution tailored for the United States today. Explain how your constitution would deal with both the original dilemma of freedom versus order and the modern dilemma of freedom versus equality.

3. America's two most important political documents, the Constitution and the Declaration of Independence, are reprinted in the back of your textbook. Both deal with the dilemma of freedom versus order. Read both documents and compare and contrast the ways they address that issue.

4. Obtain a copy of the constitution of a foreign nation (try <http://www.oefre.unibe.ch/law/icl/>) and a copy of the constitution of one of the states of the United States (try <http://www.constitution.org/cons/usstcons.htm>). Compare these to the U.S. Constitution. What similarities and differences do you find?

SAMPLE EXAM QUESTIONS

Multiple-Choice Questions

1. All of the following helped shape the design of the Constitution *except*

    a. the revolution against Britain.
    b. George Washington's warning against entangling alliances.
    c. the nation's experience under the Articles of Confederation.
    d. America's colonial past.

2. The Declaration of Independence was heavily influenced by the principles of

    a. Plato.
    b. Rousseau.
    c. Locke.
    d. Montesquieu.

3. The Declaration of Independence justified America's rebellion based on

    a. the separation of powers.
    b. the separate-but-equal doctrine.
    c. natural rights and the contract theory.
    d. divine right and the theory of concurrent majorities.

4. A government in which power is exercised by representatives who are responsible to the governed is called a

    a. republic.
    b. democracy.
    c. federation.
    d. plutocracy.

5. The Articles of Confederation

    a. established a strong central government.
    b. had no provision for amendments.
    c. provided for a weak president elected by the people.
    d. gave the central government no power to tax.

6. The founders felt they had to replace the Articles of Confederation with the Constitution because

    a. order was breaking down.
    b. freedom was limited by the central government.
    c. they wanted to construct a more majoritarian democracy.
    d. the Articles promoted inequality by allowing slavery.

7. The fact that Congress has two chambers, one in which states have equal representation and one in which state representation is based on population, is a result of the

    a. Virginia Plan.
    b. New Jersey Plan.
    c. Connecticut Compromise.
    d. Federalist Plan.

8. The Virginia Plan

    a. allowed the national legislature to nullify state laws.
    b. provided for the president to be chosen by an electoral college.
    c. was supported by small states.
    d. promoted political equality by giving access to power to the poor.

9. The compromise on the presidency provided for

   a. a two-term limit on presidential tenure.
   b. direct election by the people.
   c. presidential election and impeachment by the people.
   d. the House to choose a president if no candidate received a majority in the electoral college.

10. The principle that assigns lawmaking, law enforcing, and law interpreting to different branches of government is

    a. republicanism.
    b. federalism.
    c. separation of powers.
    d. checks and balances.

11. The three-fifths clause

    a. counted each slave as three-fifths of a person for the purpose of taxation but not representation.
    b. counted each slave as three-fifths of a person for the purpose of representation but not taxation.
    c. gave each slave a vote worth three-fifths as much as his master's vote.
    d. gave disproportionate influence in presidential elections to white men in slave states.

12. The principle that gives each branch of government some scrutiny and control over the other branches is

    a. republicanism.
    b. federalism.
    c. separation of powers.
    d. checks and balances.

13. The *Federalist* papers did all of the following *except*

    a. provide a rationale for pluralism.
    b. argue for the necessity of a bill of rights.
    c. support a strong central government.
    d. point out how checks and balances would limit tyranny.

14. Hamilton opposed the addition of a bill of rights because

    a. he wanted to increase the power of the national government over the states.
    b. a bill of rights would limit the power of the states.
    c. he believed that specifying areas where the government could not intervene might imply that it had the right to intervene in areas not listed.
    d. he was an antifederalist who wanted the Constitution to be defeated.

15. Under the U.S. Constitution, change has never come about as a result of

    a. judicial review.
    b. calling a national convention.
    c. an amendment ratified by state conventions.
    d. evolving political practice.

16. Article I grants the Congress seventeen specific powers, which together are often called

    a. implied powers.
    b. necessary and proper powers.
    c. enumerated powers.
    d. executive powers.

17. The major premise of the Declaration of Independence was that
    a.   a government's responsibility is to preserve order.
    b.   Great Britain never had a legitimate claim over the people in the colonies.
    c.   people have a right to revolt when they determine that the government is destructive of their rights.
    d.   only direct democracy is consistent with government for the American colonies.

18. The Constitution was designed primarily to
    a.   advance economic equality.
    b.   advance social equality.
    c.   create a democracy based on majority rule.
    d.   strike a balance between freedom and order.

19. Which of the following was never an issue within the Constitutional Convention of 1787?
    a.   Balancing the desire for pure democracy with the interest in a republican form of government
    b.   Finding an agreeable way to represent populations of slave and free states
    c.   Finding an agreeable way to represent large and small states
    d.   Reconciling the views of those who favored a strong national government with those wanting a looser confederation

20. The theory that states that people agree to set up rulers for certain purposes and may resist them if the rulers persistently act against those purposes is called
    a.   passive-resistance theory.
    b.   social-contract theory.
    c.   judicial review.
    d.   federal theory.

Essay Questions

1. Does the design of the Constitution promote majoritarian or pluralist politics? Explain your answer.

2. Describe the campaign to have the Constitution ratified. How did the Bill of Rights fit into that campaign?

3. How did the Constitution correct the weaknesses of the Articles of Confederation?

4. Explain how America's experience in colonial and revolutionary times influenced the design of the Constitution.

5. Explain the processes of constitutional change—both formal and informal.

ANSWERS TO MULTIPLE-CHOICE QUESTIONS

1. b
2. c
3. c
4. a
5. d
6. a
7. c
8. a
9. d
10. c
11. d
12. d
13. b
14. c
15. b
16. c
17. c
18. d
19. a
20. b

CHAPTER 3

Federalism

LEARNING OBJECTIVES

After reading this chapter you should be able to

- Define the key terms identified in the chapter margins.

- Explain why the founders adopted a federal system.

- Contrast the two competing views of federalism.

- Describe the tools used by the national government to extend its power over the states.

- Distinguish between categorical grants and block grants.

- Trace the shifting balance of power between national and state governments in the nineteenth and twentieth centuries.

- Discuss the difficulties associated with reshaping the federal system.

- Discuss the four forces that have changed the balance of power in the American federal system.

- List the main types of local government units.

- Outline the advantages and disadvantages of the federal system.

FEDERALISM AND THE CHALLENGE OF DEMOCRACY

Chapter 2 explained that the founders relied on several devices to protect freedom while providing order. One of these devices was federalism, a system that divided power between the national and state governments. Although the Constitution does specify the powers that belong to each level of government, the national government has used the elastic clause and historical circumstances to increase its power considerably. The opening vignette in Chapter 3 points out that federalism, far from being an antiquated concept relevant only to ancient history, plays an important role even in contemporary presidential elections. In the 2000 presidential election, for instance, the sovereignty of the national and state governments stood in tension, and the Supreme Court exercised its power to reverse decisions of the Florida Supreme Court.

CHAPTER OVERVIEW

Theories and Metaphors

The federal form of government was the founders' solution to the problem of making one nation out of thirteen independent states. Federalism is a form of political organization in which two or more governments exercise power and authority over the same people and territory. Federalism helped solve the problem of how to cope with diversity.

The founding of the United States gave rise to competing approaches to federalism. The first, dual federalism, emphasizes the following four points: (1) the national government may rule only by using powers specifically listed in the Constitution, (2) the national government has only limited purposes,

(3) national and state governments are sovereign in their own spheres, and (4) the relationships between the state and national governments are marked by tension. This view places importance on states' rights—the state and national governments are as distinct and separate as the layers of a cake.

The second approach, cooperative federalism, includes three elements: (1) national and state agencies perform joint functions, not just separate ones; (2) they routinely share power; and (3) power in government is fragmented rather than concentrated at one level or in one agency, so the public has many access points. The functions of the state and national governments are intermixed, like the different flavors in a marble cake. Cooperative federalists stress the Constitution's elastic clause, which has allowed the national government to stretch its powers.

Cooperative federalism has been associated with liberalism and the tendency to centralize power in the national government. Conservatives have tended to favor returning power to the states.

The Dynamics of Federalism

Although the Constitution defines the powers of the national and state governments, the actual balance of power between them has often been a matter of historical circumstances. Four specific forces have changed the relationship between the national and state governments.

The greatest changes in federalism have come in times of crisis and national emergency. In the 1930s, the power of the national government expanded enormously as President Franklin Roosevelt tried to cope with the emergency created by the Great Depression. At his request, Congress enacted a number of laws expanding the power of the federal government. Through legislation such as the Voting Rights Act of 1965, the national government forbade various practices used by the states to disenfranchise blacks. In the wake of September 11, 2001, Congress dramatically expanded the surveillance and investigative powers of the Department of Justice.

Through judicial interpretation, the Supreme Court forced state and local governments to meet demands they were otherwise unwilling or unable to meet. This was often done through the Constitution's commerce clause. During the Great Depression the Supreme Court initially held fast to a dual-federalist approach and struck down many New Deal programs. By the late 1930s, however, the Court had altered its views about the balance of power between the national and state governments and sustained acts that expanded the power of the national government. The general welfare became an accepted concern of the national government. The Court also extended the Bill of Rights to the states, outlawing segregated schools, providing minimum standards of due process, and giving expansive meaning to the commerce clause. Recently, the Court has rediscovered limits on the latitude it has given the national government.

The national government also uses financial incentives called grants-in-aid to extend its power over the states. Grants give the national government substantial power to induce states to comply with national standards. Categorical grants, targeted for special purposes, leave recipients with relatively little choice about how to spend the money; block grants, awarded for more general purposes, allow the recipient more discretion.

The fourth force shaping federalism has been the professionalization of state governments. With better education, higher salaries, more policy experience, and financial support from the federal government, state governments have emerged as sophisticated and capable policy centers.

Ideology, Policymaking, and American Federalism

Views of federalism can influence the shape of the nation's politics and policies. President Nixon's policy called New Federalism was intended to shift the balance of power from the national to the state level through the use of block grants. Between the mid-1970s and 1990, the national government's contribution to state and local spending had dropped from 25 to 17 percent. Under the Clinton administration it inched back up to 21 percent.

Although the national government now provides states with a smaller fraction of the funds they need, it still tries to tell state and local governments what to do. Since the mid-1960s, Congress has used preemption to take over functions that were previously left to the states. Preemption works through mandates (which force states to undertake activities) and restraints (which forbid states to exercise certain powers). It results in shifting costs to states for nationally imposed policies. The Republican-led 104th Congress passed legislation to limit the national government's ability to pass unfunded mandates on to the states.

Federalism and Electoral Politics

Political experience at the state level is generally crucial for entry into political office at the national level. It is not only the training and proving ground for future national politicians, but is a critical arena for building a network of contacts, die-hard constituents, and financial supporters.

Since Congressional districts are adjusted by state legislatures every ten years after the census, states have the ability to shape congressional elections. Redistricting allows legislatures to redraw district boundaries to include or exclude geographic groups of constituents. This can alter the partisan balance in a district and change the likelihood for certain types of candidates to be elected.

Federalism and the American Intergovernmental System

The American system includes more than one national and fifty state governments. Over 87,000 other governments also exercise power and authority over people living within the boundaries of the United States. Among them are municipal governments, county governments, school districts, and special districts.

Theoretically, one advantage of having so many governments is that they allow citizens the opportunity to decide their own fate in their local community, which they know intimately. However, people are less likely to participate in local elections than in national ones. A decentralized federal system gives more points of access to groups representing special interests. The multiplicity of governments also permits experimentation with new ideas and flexibility in responding to the diversity of conditions that exist around the country. But some argue that the profusion of governments makes government less comprehensible to the ordinary citizen.

Federalism and Pluralism

Both competing theories of federalism support pluralism. Both provide multiple centers of power—dual federalism by emphasizing decentralization through shifting power to the states, and cooperative federalism by stressing national standards in a political system where national officials are highly responsive to group pressures. Finally, the very existence of the federal structure encourages groups to try their luck at whichever level of government offers the best chance for success.

KEY TERMS

federalism

dual federalism

states' rights

implied powers

cooperative federalism

elastic clause

commerce clause

grant-in-aid

categorical grant

formula grant

project grant

block grant

preemption

mandate

restraint

municipal government

county government

school district

special district

RESEARCH AND RESOURCES

In addition to the websites discussed at the end of the chapter in your textbook and the selected readings grouped at the end of the textbook, you will find considerable information about the U.S. states in one of the most commonly available reference works, *The World Almanac and Book of Facts*. Good starting points for on-line research about states include *Project Vote Smart*, which features an extensive online directory of state governmental websites at <http://www.vote-smart.org/mystate_government_resources.php>. Other links to the websites of individual state governments may be found at <http://dir.yahoo.com/Government/U_S_Government/State_Government/>.

The National Council of State Legislatures provides information, research on critical state issues, publications, and a voice in Washington, D.C., for state legislators across the country. See <http://www.ncsl.org/>.

USING YOUR KNOWLEDGE

1. Pick up the most current volume of *The World Almanac and Book of Facts* and look up the word *states* to get a sense of the comparative data available on a state-by-state basis. Next, select four states in different parts of the country and profile each using a common set of characteristics you suspect might have political importance. (For example, you might look at net migration, ethnicity of population, indicators that show the importance of industry or agriculture, military contracts, and so on.)

2. Interview someone who has moved to your state from another state. What are the major differences he or she has noticed? Are these differences political, legal, economic, or social? See if you are able to find data to substantiate your interviewee's impressions.

3. Tour the websites of five state governments. Compare and contrast the types of information they make available.

GETTING INVOLVED

One of the great advantages of pluralist democracy is that it provides lots of opportunities for you to get involved. If you would like to learn more about the inner workings of government, you need not go to Washington, D.C. With over 87,000 governments in our system, possibilities for internships are bound to be available right in your own backyard in state and local government. It is not possible to provide detailed information for all fifty states, but here are a few examples of what's out there.

Like their Washington counterpart, several state legislatures have internships available. In Indiana, for example, the Democratic and Republican caucuses in each house of the state legislature offer internships to students who help during the legislative session. In addition, the caucuses sometimes help place internship candidates in positions with interest groups or think tanks in the area. Other states such as Florida, Illinois, Michigan, Minnesota, Montana, New York, and Rhode Island also offer internships.

Finally, many cities (including Oakland, California; Phoenix, Arizona; New York City; Detroit; and Los Angeles) offer internship possibilities. Try calling the local government personnel office in your own area to find out what's available near you.

Obtaining an internship is much like getting a job. You can begin the search with a simple phone call to your state legislator's office to inquire whether they offer internships. If so, ask whether there is a particular application procedure. Some offices have a specific application form to fill out, while others might simply ask you to submit a letter explaining your interest and a resume. Interviews are common, because they give the office an opportunity to evaluate your maturity, professionalism, and communications skills. Although there are exceptions, remember that the vast majority of political internships are unpaid.

SAMPLE EXAM QUESTIONS

Multiple-Choice Questions

1. The concept of "states' rights" is most commonly associated with
    a. marble-cake federalism.
    b. cooperative federalism.
    c. layer-cake federalism.
    d. new federalism.
2. Cooperative federalism emphasizes
    a. a readily expandable elastic clause.
    b. the layer-cake metaphor.
    c. states' rights.
    d. the Tenth Amendment as a limit on the national government.
3. Dual federalism accepts all of the following principles *except*
    a. the claim that the national government rules by enumerated powers only.
    b. recognition of the dynamic purposes of the national government.
    c. separate spheres of sovereignty for national and state governments.
    d. a relationship between national and state governments characterized by tension.
4. The quality of being supreme in power or authority is
    a. sovereignty.
    b. cooperative federalism.
    c. new federalism.
    d. dual federalism.
5. The elastic or necessary-and-proper clause of the Constitution has been used by cooperative federalists to
    a. limit the power of the national government.
    b. enhance the power of state governments.
    c. promote interaction between the levels of government.
    d. protect state sovereignty.

6. The balance of power between the state and national governments has been affected by

    a. national crises.
    b. judicial interpretation.
    c. federal grant money.
    d. All of the above.

7. Categorical grants

    a. leave little discretion to recipient governments.
    b. never require state or local governments to match funds.
    c. are awarded on the basis of politically neutral formulas.
    d. are being phased out in favor of revenue sharing.

8. The Supreme Court's reaction to Franklin Roosevelt's New Deal legislation was to

    a. accept it immediately.
    b. reject it as unconstitutional.
    c. initially accept it, but later reverse themselves and rule it unconstitutional.
    d. initially reject it as unconstitutional, but later reverse themselves and accept it.

9. The Supreme Court case that upheld the doctrines of national supremacy and implied powers was

    a. *Marbury* v. *Madison*.
    b. *McCulloch* v. *Maryland*.
    c. *United States* v. *Butler*.
    d. *Hammer* v. *Dagenhart*.

10. In *Prinz* v. *United States*, the Supreme Court ruled that the federal government could

    a. require local law enforcement officials to implement background checks.
    b. not require local police officers to implement a federal regulatory scheme.
    c. not ban the possession of a gun in or near a school.
    d. establish speed limits on federal highways.

11. In *United States* v. *Lopez*, the Supreme Court ruled that the federal government could

    a. require local law enforcement officials to implement background checks.
    b. not require local police officers to implement a federal regulatory scheme.
    c. not ban the possession of a gun in or near a school.
    d. establish speed limits on federal highways.

12. The authors note that the main constitutional authority for the Voting Rights Act of 1965 came primarily from

    a. the elastic clause.
    b. the Fifteenth Amendment.
    c. the Twenty-Fourth Amendment.
    d. None of the above.

13. Pre-emption has involved the use of

    a. mandates.
    b. restraints.
    c. cost shifting to states.
    d. All of the above.

14. The principal technique used by the national government to establish a uniform drinking age was

    a. a constitutional amendment.
    b. a mandate requiring states to change the drinking age and giving them no choice.
    c. pre-emption transferring the authority for setting the drinking age to the national government.
    d. legislation reducing highway grants to states that did not set their drinking age at twenty-one.

15. The level of professionalization in state governments has

  a. increased in the last 40 years, strengthening their policymaking capability.
  b. declined over the last 40 years, weakening the states compared to the federal governmnet.
  c. declined over the last 40 years, despite impressive gains in the educational levels of state employees.
  d. not changed noticeably over the last 40 years.

16. Throughout U.S. history, the Supreme Court's interpretation of federalism has

  a. always been broad.
  b. always been narrow.
  c. varied considerably.
  d. had little impact on relations between the state and national governments.

17. The Elementary and Secondary Education Act of 1965

  a. had several provisions that strengthened state governments' ability to administer programs.
  b. marked the end of national support for local educational programs.
  c. outlawed the expenditure of federal funds on disadvantaged students.
  d. was ruled unconstitutional two years later because it allowed states to act in an enumerated federal domain.

18. The Tenth Amendment to the Constitution asserts that

  a. Congress shall make no law prohibiting the free exercise of religion.
  b. slavery shall be outlawed in the United States.
  c. no state shall deny any person due process of law.
  d. the powers not explicitly granted to the national government are reserved for the states or the people.

19. Which of the following Court actions has led to an expansion of national government power?

  a. The interpretation of the commerce clause of the Constitution
  b. The extension of the Bill of Rights to the states under the Fourteenth Amendment
  c. The decision in *McCulloch* v. *Maryland*
  d. All of the above

20. The Voting Rights Act of 1965 is an example of the use of

  a. legislative sanctions to compel behavior conforming to nationally set standards.
  b. judicial review to compel behavior conforming to nationally set standards.
  c. legislative incentives to reward behavior.
  d. legislative power to increase states' rights.

Essay Questions

1. Explain the two competing views of federalism.

2. Discuss the factors that have led to the growth of the national government's power.

3. What was the significance of *McCulloch* v. *Maryland* for the development of U.S. federalism? Has the Court always decided in favor of expanding the national government's power? Give examples.

4. What are the advantages and disadvantages of a federal system?

ANSWERS TO MULTIPLE-CHOICE QUESTIONS

1. c
2. a
3. b
4. a
5. c
6. d
7. a
8. d
9. b
10. b
11. c
12. b
13. d
14. d
15. a
16. c
17. a
18. d
19. d
20. a

CHAPTER 4

Public Opinion, Political Socialization, and the Media

LEARNING OBJECTIVES

After reading this chapter you should be able to

- Define the key terms identified in the chapter margins.

- Contrast the majoritarian and pluralist models of democracy with respect to their assumptions about public opinion.

- List several agents of political socialization and describe their impact.

- Show how social or demographic characteristics (such as education, income, ethnicity, region, religion, and so forth) are linked to political values.

- Analyze how the two-dimensional typology of political ideology presented in Chapter 1 applies to the actual distribution of political opinions among Americans.

- Outline the technological changes and events that have influenced the development of the media in the United States.

- Explain who owns the media in the United States and how the government regulates them.

- Discuss the consequences of private ownership of the media.

- Explain how people acquire news through the media.

- Describe how the mass media contribute to political socialization.

- Indicate the ways in which the mass media influence political behavior.

- Assess the validity of the charges of media bias.

- Evaluate the contribution the media make to democratic government.

PUBLIC OPINION, POLITICAL SOCIALIZATION, THE MEDIA, AND THE CHALLENGE OF DEMOCRACY

This chapter's opening vignette contrasts public attitudes toward punishment in the United States with practices under the former Taliban government of Afghanistan. To maintain a high degree of order and a low crime rate, the Taliban beheaded, stoned, and dismembered offenders. Although a majority of Americans favor capital punishment, American public opinion would not tolerate the kinds of grisly punishments accepted as a matter of course by the Taliban. Americans are willing to tolerate more disorder. Public opinion thus places boundaries on allowable types of public policy.

Yet, American attitudes themselves do change over time. Specifically, Americans are more likely to favor capital punishment during periods when the social order is threatened (for instance, by war, foreign subversion, or crime). Furthermore, as support for capital punishment has weakened, the

Supreme Court has deemed unconstitutional the execution of mentally retarded individuals and individuals who were minors when they committed their offense.

An examination of people's opinions on the clashes between freedom and order and freedom and equality shows that the public really does divide itself into the four ideological categories suggested in Chapter 1. Furthermore, the four groups differ in terms of their socioeconomic and demographic characteristics.

The nature of public opinion is particularly important to the distinction between the pluralist and majoritarian models of democracy. These models differ in their assumptions about the role of public opinion. Majoritarians depend on an informed public with stable opinions acting to guide public policy. They believe government should do what the public wants. Pluralists, on the other hand, do not expect the general public to demonstrate much knowledge or display stable or consistent opinions. Consequently, pluralists doubt that majority opinion can provide a guide for public policy. Instead, they depend on interested and knowledgeable subgroups to compete in an open process to achieve public policy goals.

Opinion research certainly shows that the majoritarian assumptions about knowledge do not describe the public as a whole. Yet, lack of knowledge itself does not prevent people from expressing an opinion on an issue. However, when knowledge and interest concerning an issue both are low, public opinion is likely to be changing and unstable. Groups that are highly interested in an issue do have more opportunity to make an impact, yet such groups are often directly opposed by other groups. Politically powerful groups disagree on what they want government to do. As a result, politicians have a great deal of leeway in deciding what policies to pursue. And as the opening vignette points out, although the government tends to react to public opinion, it does not always do what the people want.

The mass media link the people and the government by making possible a two-way flow of information. The media report government actions to the people, and they also poll the public to assess people's opinions on specific issues. Although both of these functions are critically important to the majoritarian model of democracy, pluralist democracy relies on more specialized channels of communication.

For a pluralist system to be democratic, however, open channels of access are necessary. Although the government originally regulated the airwaves simply to provide order, later government limitations on the freedom of broadcasters have helped provide greater equality of access to the airwaves. Through government regulation, the electronic media have been required to present opposing points of view. In recent years, the media became more of a free market. The Telecommunications Act of 1996 relaxed many restrictions on media ownership, thus allowing for greater concentration of the media in a limited number of hands. This promotes freedom, but it limits equality. On the other hand, in terms of coverage of events over the years, the media have tended to promote social equality. This trend can be seen in coverage of the civil rights and women's movements.

The freedom issue of greatest interest to the media, not surprisingly, has been the question of freedom of expression. Yet, as this chapter indicates, the development of the Internet has posed a number of new challenges to the ability of a government to ensure order. This form of media is international, and content "published" on the Internet in one country is available abroad. Publishing on the Internet, as in other forms of media, can create a tension between freedom and order (most dramatically when material banned in one country is placed on the Internet by servers in another country). To accept any one value as absolute means paying a high price, and that is clearly the case with freedom of the press.

CHAPTER OVERVIEW

Public Opinion and Models of Democracy

Public opinion is defined as the collective attitude of the citizenry on a given issue or question. Pluralists and majoritarians differ on the role of public opinion in a democracy. Majoritarians believe the government should do what the majority of the public wants. Pluralists think the opinion of the general public is not very clear or settled but that subgroups may have very well-developed opinions that must be allowed to be openly asserted if democracy is to function.

Modern polling techniques developed over the last fifty years now make it possible to find out what the people's attitudes are—and also to discover when the government fails to follow the public's wishes, as the majoritarian model stipulates.

Political Socialization

Public opinion is rooted in political values, which are produced in turn through a process of political socialization. Early political socialization comes from one's family and school, as well as peer and community groups. Among adults, peer groups and mass media play a particularly influential role in the ongoing process of socialization.

Social Groups and Political Values

People with similar backgrounds often share various learning experiences, and they tend to develop similar political opinions. Background factors generally believed to affect political opinions include education, income, region, ethnicity, religion, and gender. The impact of these factors may change over time. After the civil war, for example, African Americans were initially mobilized by the Republican Party, which was associated with Abraham Lincoln. By the 1930s and 1940s, however, they were associating with Franklin Roosevelt's New Deal Democratic coalition.

From Values to Ideology

Although early surveys showed relatively little ideological thinking on the part of voters, some subsequent research has shown more ideological awareness. Most voters are willing to place themselves on a liberal-to-conservative continuum; however, they often lack the consistent values and beliefs about the scope and purpose of government that characterize truly ideological thinking.

When people are asked to describe liberals and conservatives, they seldom employ political terms. Rather, survey respondents characterize liberals as "open-minded" and "free-spending," while they label conservatives "fiscally responsible or tight" and "close-minded." When people are asked about their own attitudes on these issues, they separate into four groups, not two. This suggests that the liberal-conservative ideological framework oversimplifies matters and that ideology is not one-dimensional. By examining where they stand on two areas of conflict—freedom versus order and freedom versus equality—Americans may be divided into four ideological types: liberals, conservatives, communitarians, and libertarians. (This is the same typology introduced in Chapter 1.) People with similar socioeconomic and demographic characteristics also often share the same ideological outlook. Minorities and people with less education and low incomes are often communitarians. Libertarians tend to have more education and higher incomes. Conservatives are more common in the Midwest, and liberals are more common in the Northeast.

The Process of Forming Political Opinions

A minority of citizens form their political opinions around ideology; most citizens rely on other factors. This chapter considers three of them: political knowledge, self-interest, political leadership.

Americans have many sources of political information, yet their political knowledge and level of political sophistication tend to be low. Researchers suggest that political knowledge is correlated with education levels, and public opinions are often highly changeable when based upon little knowledge. Although self-interest is often the dominant influence on opinions about economic matters and matters of social equality, there are many issues for which personal benefit is not a factor.

Finally, political leaders also influence the formation of public opinion. Favorable or unfavorable evaluations of a politician may shape public opinion concerning the politician's proposals. Furthermore, the ability of political leaders to affect public opinion has been enhanced by the growth of the broadcast media.

The Media in America

The media include the technical devices and processes used in mass communication that allow individuals or groups to transmit information to large, heterogeneous, widely dispersed audiences. Today, the mass media used in political communication include *print media*, such as newspapers and magazines, and *broadcast media*, such as television, radio, and the Internet. In democratic governments, the mass media promote a two-way flow of communication between citizens and the government.

The Internet. The last quarter century witnessed the introduction of new technologies that have been used for political communications between groups with common interests. The most significant of these is the Internet. The Internet makes information readily available and also allows users to share their opinions internationally for a relatively low cost.

Private Ownership of the Media. In the United States, both the print and electronic media are privately owned. While this gives the news industry great political freedom, it also means that news is selected for its audience appeal, as judged by its impact on readers or listeners; its sensationalism; its treatment of familiar people or life situations; its close-to-home character; or its timeliness.

Ownership of the media in the United States has become more and more concentrated, as the same corporations control many newspapers and radio and television stations.

Government Regulation of the Media. The broadcast media operate under the regulations of an independent regulatory commission, the Federal Communications Commission (FCC). The FCC licenses broadcasters using the airwaves in the public interest. Broadcasters are required to provide reasonable access to community groups with differing viewpoints, and any broadcaster that gives or sells time to a political candidate must make equal access to all other candidates in that race under the same conditions.

Reporting and Following the News

The news media serve five specific functions for the political system: (1) reporting the news, (2) interpreting the news, (3) influencing citizens' opinions, (4) setting the agenda for government action, and (5) socializing citizens about politics. Their reporters may rely on news releases, news briefings, press conferences, leaks, and cultivation of background sources for their material. The tendency for news reporters to be grouped together in pressrooms and to rely on the same sources of information has given rise to a style of reporting sometimes referred to as pack journalism.

Since the 1960s, people have reported that they get more of their news from television than from any other source. However, studies have suggested that many people are news "grazers" who check the news from time to time rather than following the news steadily. Because television often relies on short sound bites and visual images, supporters of the "television hypothesis" suggest that television is to blame for Americans' low level of political knowledge. However, television seems to convey certain types of information better than the print media.

People believe that the media influence public opinion, and some studies have shown systematic and dramatic opinion changes linked to television news coverage, particularly to policy positions taken by news commentators. Nevertheless, most scholars believe that the real power of the media consists of their ability to set the national agenda. Through the kind of stories they cover, the media help define the issues that get government attention.

The media also act as agents of political socialization. In this regard, their role is often contradictory. On the one hand, they contribute to American self-confidence by supporting public celebrations as great media events; on the other hand, they give air time to events and activities that reduce the sense of national well-being. The entertainment divisions may promote the values of law-abiding citizens, or they may do the reverse.

Evaluating the Media in Government

Media executives function as gatekeepers, deciding which stories to report and how to handle them. Any selection process reflects something about the values of the selector, and in the case of the media, the process often leads to charges of media bias. News reporters have been criticized for liberal bias, while media owners are often charged with having a conservative bias. Yet, one researcher has found no continuing bias on the television news, except against incumbents and front-runners.

In general, the media improve the quality of information citizens receive about the government. They report public opinion. These functions help make responsible government possible.

The media have mobilized government action to advance racial and sexual equality. They also uphold the value of freedom when the freedom in question is freedom of the press. Yet, press freedom may conflict with order and thus, like all democratic values, is not without its costs to society.

KEY TERMS

public opinion

political socialization

socioeconomic status

self-interest principle

mass media

newsworthiness

Federal Communications Commission (FCC)

equal opportunities rule

reasonable access rule

gatekeepers

horse race journalism

television hypothesis

political agenda

RESEARCH AND RESOURCES

Gathering Data on Public Opinion. No doubt you are already familiar with a number of public opinion polls. Newspapers, magazines, and television news broadcasts often present information gathered through public-opinion polling. Well-known polls include those done by the Harris and Roper organizations, ABC News/*New York Times* polls, CBS News/*Washington Post* polls, and, of course, the Gallup Poll. Data from these polls are often available to the public. The Gallup Organization, for example, puts out a monthly publication giving the results of its surveys. Periodically, these surveys are indexed and bound in permanent volumes, which can be found in the reference sections of most college libraries. You can find Gallup on-line at <http://www.gallup.com/>. Many university libraries subscribe to the Gallup Poll either in print or electronic format.

Are you ready to become part of the attentive public? Why not get to know the public affairs magazines that help shape American opinion? The *Reader's Guide to Periodical Literature* will help you find these publications. Many of them have Web sites where you can sample what they have to offer.

When you use publications for information, you should be aware that magazines often have an explicit or implicit ideological orientation. Certain publications present views from the American left; others give the opinions of those on the right. If you are trying to examine an issue thoroughly, you will probably want to weigh arguments from each side. So it is important to make sure that not all of your background material comes from right-wing or left-wing publications. Some important journals of opinion include the following.

On the right:

> *National Review.* William F. Buckley's magazine, a long-time standard-bearer of conservative ideas. <http://www.nationalreview.com/>

> *The Public Interest.* Conservative, but not given to polemics. <http://www.thepublicinterest.com>

> *Commentary.* This monthly, sponsored by a national Jewish organization, was once listed among the nation's liberal publications. But its hard-line stands on foreign-policy issues under the present editor, Norman Podhoretz, now move it more toward the conservative side.

> *The Weekly Standard.* A conservative publication that debuted in 1995. <http://www.weeklystandard.com>

Somewhere in the center, generally striving for editorial balance:

> *The Atlantic Monthly.* A monthly publication that includes several lengthy articles each month on aspects of U.S. foreign or domestic policy. <http://www.TheAtlantic.com/>

> *Daedalus.* An academic quarterly; each volume focuses on a single topic and offers a variety of viewpoints.

> *Harper's.* Similar to *Atlantic,* it now includes readings excerpted from other works and a wonderful list of offbeat facts in the front of each issue. <http://www.harpers.org/>

On the left:

> *The New Republic.* A leading liberal periodical that has moved more to the right in recent years; highly opinionated and often acerbic. <http://www.thenewrepublic.com/>

> *The Nation.* The oldest continuously published journal of opinion in the country; it covers wide-ranging political topics. <http://www.TheNation.com/>

> *The Progressive.* Another venerable and respected journal of liberal thought.

And finally, some on-line addresses for "alternative" publications to explore:

> *Mother Jones* <http://www.mojones.com/>

> *The Utne Reader* <http://www.utne.com/>

USING YOUR KNOWLEDGE

1. Locate the Gallup Poll volumes in the reference section of your library. Using the index, find the polls taken on the issue of abortion during any five years from 1969 to the present. Make a graph showing the opinion distribution of the sample as a whole for each poll you find. Make a line graph showing the percentage selecting "favor" in each of these polls. Is the opinion distribution stable or unstable over time?

2. Using the data you gathered in Exercise 1, look at the opinions of the subgroups (religion, age, region, or whatever) and compare these opinions to the average opinion for the sample as a whole. Does opinion in any of the subgroups shift over time?

3. Select one of the following controversial subjects: welfare, abortion, or immigration. Using the *Reader's Guide to Periodical Literature* and the Internet resources listed above, locate three or four articles on your topic in various magazines that have different ideological slants. Skim the articles. Are the opinions expressed in the articles consistent with the ideological orientations of the publications as described in the lists above?

4. Watch a television news broadcast and select the major political story covered. Compare the television coverage of that event or issue with newspaper accounts of the same story. What are the differences and similarities in the two accounts?

5. Many television news services have established on-line links. Watch the television news program and then check out the on-line service. For example, try the all-news station MSNBC and then visit their Web site at <http://www.msnbc.msn.com>. How does using the Web site affect your political knowledge?

6. What is the difference between "conventional" and "unconventional" media? Compare the treatment of a major political news story on *Larry King Live* (on-line at <http://www.cnn.com/CNN/Programs/larry.king.live/>) with coverage of the same issue on the PBS *NewsHour with Jim Lehrer* (on-line at <http://www.pbs.org/newshour/>) or the Sunday morning news programs such as *Meet the Press* (on-line at <http://www.msnbc.msn.com/id/3032608/>).

GETTING INVOLVED

Students who want to learn more about the media from the inside may be interested in applying for internships with broadcasters, newspapers, magazines, or other media-related organizations. Here are a few of the opportunities available. Some may require previous experience in journalism, such as work on your college newspaper.

C-SPAN <http://www.cspan.org/> has internships for students interested in communications and politics. Students must meet three basic criteria: they must be a college junior or senior, they must be interning for college credit, and they must be able to work a minimum of sixteen hours per week. Resumès can be submitted online at <http://www.recruitingcenter.net/clients/cspan/publicjobs/>.

The Center for Investigative Reporting, a nonprofit, independent organization committed to investigative reporting, offers five-month paid internships to students who want to pair off with senior reporters and learn the techniques of investigative journalism. For winter/spring internships, the deadline is December 1; for summer/fall, it is May 1. For more information, see <http://www.muckraker.org/jobs_internships.php> or write: The Center for Investigative Reporting, attn: Internship Coordinator, 131 Stuart Street, Suite 600, San Francisco, CA 94105.

The *Los Angeles Times* hires interns for its California offices as well as one intern for its Washington bureau. Summer internships are eleven weeks long, with a December 1 application deadline; part-time internships lasting seventeen weeks are available in the fall and spring, with June 1 and October 1 deadlines, respectively. Address: The *Los Angeles Times,* Editorial Internships, Times Mirror Square, Los Angeles, CA 90053. On-line site: <http://www.latimes.com/>.

The *Philadelphia Inquirer* offers paid summer internships in reporting. Internships run from Memorial Day to late August. Applications are due in mid-January. For further information, contact: Acel Moore, Philadelphia Inquirer, Box 8263, Philadelphia, PA 19101. Questions may be sent to recruiting@phillynews.com. On-line site: <http://www.philly.com/mld/inquirer/>.

The *Boston Globe* offers full-time paid work to interns from June 1 to Labor Day. The program also includes seminars on legal issues, constitutional issues, and other issues related to journalism. The application deadline is December 1. For further information, contact: The *Boston Globe,* Boston, MA 02107. Telephone: (617) 929-2000. On-line site: <http://www.boston.com/globe/>.

The *Washington Post* offers summer internships to current college juniors and seniors interested in journalism. Application deadline is November 1. For further information, contact: Summer Internship Program, News Department, The *Washington Post,* 1150 15th Street, NW, Washington, DC 20071-5508. Telephone: (202) 334-6000. On-line site: <http://washpost.com/news_ed/summer_internships/index.shtml>.

The *Atlantic Monthly* offers students an opportunity to work at an award-winning national magazine. Contact: Lucie Prinz, The *Atlantic Monthly,* 77 North Washington, Boston, MA 02114. On-line site: <http://www.theatlantic.com/a/intern.mhtml>.

Harper's Magazine offers unpaid, full-time internships in spring, summer, and fall. Deadlines are October 15, February 15, and June 15, respectively. For further information, contact: Internship Coordinator, *Harper's Magazine,* 666 Broadway, 11th Floor, New York, NY 10012. (212) 420-5720. On-line site: <http://www.harpers.org/HarpersInternships.html>.

SAMPLE EXAM QUESTIONS

Multiple-Choice Questions

1. Public opinion on the death penalty reveals which characteristic about public opinion?
    a.   Americans strongly oppose the death penalty.
    b.   The public's attitude toward a public policy can vary over time.
    c.   Citizens will not express opinions about issues on which they are uninformed.
    d.   The public's attitude toward a public policy will not change over time.
2. Socialization is defined as
    a.   the process of acquiring political values.
    b.   adopting Marxist tendencies.
    c.   conversing with friends about politics.
    d.   a method of conducting public opinion polls.
3. The primary elements of early socialization generally include all *except*
    a.   family.
    b.   school experience.
    c.   newspapers.
    d.   television.
4. The more educated people are, the
    a.   more likely they are to favor redistribution of income.
    b.   more likely they are to think abortion should be a matter of a woman's choice.
    c.   less likely they are to value freedom over order.
    d.   less tolerant they are of dissent.

5.   In general, African Americans and Latinos tend to

   a.   favor restrictions on abortion.
   b.   oppose restrictions on abortion.
   c.   share the socioeconomic status and political views of Asians.
   d.   favor government action to improve economic opportunity.

6.   In the United States, communitarians tend to be prominent

   a.   among people with low education and income.
   b.   among people with high education and income.
   c.   in the West.
   d.   in the Northeast.

7.   Women are less supportive than men of all the following *except*

   a.   going to war.
   b.   government spending for social programs.
   c.   the death penalty.
   d.   the Republican Party.

8.   The set of values and beliefs that people hold about the purpose and scope of government are called

   a.   ideologies.
   b.   libertarians.
   c.   opinion distributions.
   d.   opinion shapes.

9.   If given the range of choices below, most Americans would probably classify themselves as

   a.   liberal.
   b.   moderate.
   c.   conservative.
   d.   libertarian.

10.   Which religious group tends to be the most conservative on social issues?

   a.   Protestants
   b.   Catholics
   c.   Jews
   d.   There are no noticeable differences between these groups.

11.   Despite the fact that American education levels are high and political information is available,

   a.   Americans are reluctant to offer their opinions on political matters.
   b.   Americans are lacking in political knowledge.
   c.   Americans base most of their political decisions on clearly defined ideological positions.
   d.   there is no link between education and political sophistication.

12.   A democracy is best served by the media when they

   a.   allow for a two-way flow of information.
   b.   allow for a one-way flow of information.
   c.   emphasize the entertainment value of news.
   d.   do not attempt to reflect popular views.

13.   The authors refer to the Internet as a form of

   a.   print media.
   b.   global media.
   c.   broadcast media.
   d.   episodic media.

14. Ownership concentration in the media

    a.   has been increasing.
    b.   was tightly limited by the FCC under the 1996 Telecommunications Act.
    c.   occurs only within specific media industries.
    d.   has been avoided in the United States through private ownership of the media.

15. Which of the following is *not* a consequence of private ownership of the broadcast media?

    a.   Media dependence on advertising
    b.   Media attention to ratings
    c.   Media selection of stories based primarily on political significance
    d.   Media emphasis on entertainment value in the presentation of news

16. Most Americans rely on which of the following as their chief news source?

    a.   Newspapers
    b.   Magazines
    c.   Radio
    d.   Television

17. Which of the following characteristics is linked to news grazers?

    a.   Youth
    b.   Race
    c.   Gender
    d.   Education

18. Television today promotes popular support for government through

    a.   programs like *The X-Files* and *NYPD Blue.*
    b.   coverage of protests.
    c.   coverage of celebrations of national holidays.
    d.   horse race journalism.

19. The ability for journalists to make decisions about which issues to cover, thereby thrusting concerns onto the public agenda is known as

    a.   gatekeeping.
    b.   a feeding frenzy.
    c.   pack journalism.
    d.   yellow journalism.

20. Mass media are

    a.   more important in the pluralist than in the majoritarian model of democracy.
    b.   more important in the majoritarian than in the pluralist model of democracy.
    c.   equally important to each model.
    d.   unimportant in totalitarian states.

21. The value most likely to be held as absolute by the media is

    a.   freedom of expression.
    b.   equality of access.
    c.   social order.
    d.   liberalism.

22. The FCC's equal opportunities rule requires that

    a.   a station that sells time to one candidate for public office must sell it to other candidates for that office under the same conditions.
    b.   stations must hire women and minorities in news anchor positions.
    c.   stations must carry news of interest to each ethnic group in the community.
    d.   minorities should receive additional opportunities to purchase television licenses.

23. In judging the newsworthiness of a story, the primary criterion used is
    a. political significance.
    b. audience appeal.
    c. educational value.
    d. broad social importance.
24. The television hypothesis suggests that
    a. television is the most effective means for following the actions of public officials.
    b. television is the most effective medium to convey information about complex topics.
    c. television has lowered the campaign costs for candidates running for public office.
    d. television is to blame for the low level of citizens' knowledge about public affairs.
25. The reasonable access rule required broadcasters to
    a. make their stations accessible to wheelchair users.
    b. discuss public issues and provide fair coverage to each side on an issue.
    c. make equal time available on the same terms to all candidates for an office.
    d. make their facilities available for the expression of conflicting views by responsible elements of the community.

Essay Questions

1. Compare the pluralist and majoritarian models in their assumptions about public opinion. Which model is closer to American political reality?

2. How are race and religion related to political values?

3. Discuss the limitations of the one-dimensional liberal-conservative typology of political ideology. How does the liberal-conservative typology compare to the fourfold classification developed in Chapters 1 and 4?

4. Evaluate the effectiveness of television as a source of political information for the general public.

5. Are the national news media biased? Answer this question by discussing research outlined in the chapter.

6. What are the consequences of private ownership of the media? Explain how concentration of media ownership might undermine democratic government.

7. Discuss the strengths and limitations of media influence on political behavior.

ANSWERS TO MULTIPLE-CHOICE QUESTIONS

1. b
2. a
3. c
4. b
5. a
6. a
7. b
8. a
9. b
10. a
11. b
12. a
13. c
14. a
15. c
16. d
17. a
18. c
19. a
20. b
21. a
22. a
23. b
24. d
25. d

CHAPTER 5

Participation and Voting

LEARNING OBJECTIVES

After reading this chapter you should be able to

- Define the key terms identified in the chapter margins.

- Distinguish between conventional and unconventional participation.

- Explain the difference between particularized participation and activities geared to influence broad policy.

- Compare American political participation with participation in other democracies.

- Discuss the extension of suffrage to blacks, women, and eighteen-year-olds.

- Explain the nature of initiatives, referendums, and recalls.

- Account for the low voter turnout in the United States.

- Evaluate the extent to which various forms of political participation enhance freedom, order, or equality.

- Assess the extent to which the various forms of participation fit the pluralist or majoritarian model of democracy.

PARTICIPATION, VOTING, AND THE CHALLENGE OF DEMOCRACY

Free participation in democracy means citizens must be given the choice to participate or not to participate. It also means they may use the resources at their disposal to try to influence the government. Freedom thus favors those who have the most resources to advance their interests. Equal participation means every citizen's ability to influence government should be equal to every other citizen's, so that a lack of personal resources does not work to the disadvantage of anyone.

At one time in the United States, safeguarding order meant restricting participation. It meant not letting certain groups (women and blacks) vote for fear of upsetting the social order. Today, protecting order may mean opening up the political process so that groups have less incentive to engage in unconventional participation.

The most obvious function of elections is to allow citizens to choose among candidates or issues. In addition, elections also socialize political activity, institutionalize mass influence in politics, regularize access to power, and bolster the state's power and authority.

The majoritarian model assumes that government responds to popular wishes articulated through conventional channels, primarily voting in elections. The majoritarians count each vote equally and are hence biased toward the value of equality in participation. By emphasizing conventional participation, majoritarians come to resemble populists.

The pluralist model emphasizes freedom. Citizens are free to use all their resources to influence government at any of the many access points available to them. Thus, organizations such as militia groups have made extensive use of group media. Pluralism may seem to favor those with resources, but in contrast to majoritarianism, it allows plenty of room for unconventional political participation. Yet, when people are forced to rely on unconventional participation to be heard, it is hard to call the system democratic.

CHAPTER OVERVIEW

Democracy and Political Participation

Voting is central to democracy, but when voting is the only form of participation available, there is no real democracy. In addition to casting votes, citizens must also be able to discuss politics, form interest groups, contact public officials, campaign for competing parties, run for office, or protest government decisions, for example.

Political participation—the actions of private citizens that are intended to influence or support government or politics—may be either conventional or unconventional.

Unconventional Participation

Unconventional participation is relatively uncommon behavior that challenges the government and is personally stressful to participants and their opponents. Unconventional acts might include protest demonstrations, boycotts, blocking traffic, and so forth. Terrorism is an extreme form of unconventional participation. Unconventional participation, such as the Selma march that led to the passage of the Voting Rights Act of 1965, is often difficult but occasionally pays off.

Despite a tradition dating back to the Boston Tea Party, unconventional participation is frowned on by most Americans, especially when it disrupts their daily life. Yet, Americans are more likely to engage in unconventional political participation than are citizens of other democratic states. Researchers find unconventional participation hard to study but suggest that groups resort to unconventional participation precisely because they are powerless and have been denied access to conventional channels of participation. Despite the public's belief that unconventional participation is generally ineffective, direct political action sometimes works. Unconventional actions such as protests and marches tend to appeal to those who distrust the political system, have a strong sense of political efficacy, and manage to develop a sense of group consciousness.

Conventional Participation

The comparatively high rate of unconventional political participation presents a dilemma for U.S. democracy because the whole point of democratic politics is to make political participation conventional. Conventional political behavior includes (1) actions that show support for government, such as participating in patriotic celebrations, and (2) actions that try to change or influence government policies, either to secure personal benefits or to achieve broad policy objectives.

Attempts to achieve broad policy objectives include activities that require little initiative (voting) and those that require high initiative (attending meetings, persuading others how to vote, attending congressional hearings, running for office, etc.). People also participate by using the court system (for example, by joining in class-action suits). Americans are less likely to vote than citizens in other democracies, but they are at least as likely to participate in other conventional ways.

Participation Through Voting

In the United States, the right to vote was extended only gradually to various groups (blacks, women, eighteen-year-olds). For much of its history, the United States departed considerably from the democratic ideal; yet, in comparison with other countries, the United States has a good record of providing for equality in voting rights.

In addition to selecting candidates for office, citizens of some states vote on issues by means of referenda and initiatives, two devices not available on the national level. These help representative democracy more closely resemble direct democracy, but they are not without drawbacks. For one thing, they are quite expensive; for another, referendum campaigns often increase rather than decrease the impact of special-interest groups. Many states also provide for recalls, or special elections, to remove an officeholder.

Voting for candidates is the most visible form of political participation. It serves democratic government by allowing citizens to choose the candidates they think would make the best public officials and then to hold officials accountable for their actions in government, by either re-electing or removing them. This assumes citizens are knowledgeable about what officials do and participate actively by going to the polls.

The United States holds more elections and has more offices subject to election than do other countries. However, American participation in elections is very low compared with that of other democracies.

Explaining Political Participation

Not only is voter turnout in the United States comparatively low, it has also declined over time. However, other forms of participation are high and are stable or on the increase.

Conventional participation is often related to socioeconomic status. The higher a person's education, income, or occupational status, the more likely he or she is to vote or use other conventional means to influence government. On the other hand, unconventional participation is less clearly related to socioeconomic status. Over the years, race, sex, and marital status have been related to participation in the United States. But the single most influential factor affecting conventional participation is education.

Arguments now advanced to explain the decline in voter turnout point to the influx of new, young voters enfranchised under the Twenty-Sixth Amendment. Young voters are less likely to vote. Other reasons offered include the growing belief that the government is unresponsive to citizens and the decline in people's identification with a political party.

Another possible explanation for the low U.S. turnout is that it is more difficult to vote here than in other countries. In the United States, citizens are required to register in advance, which leaves the initiative up to the individual citizen. Registration requirements work to reduce the number of people actually eligible to vote on election day. The "motor voter" law made it easier to register and was expected to increase participation. However, its impact is not yet clear. A final explanation for low turnout is that, although the act of voting is relatively simple, learning about candidates takes a great deal of initiative, and many eligible to vote may feel inadequate to the task.

Participation and Freedom, Equality, and Order

Whereas the relationships between participation and freedom and between participation and equality are clear, the relationship between participation and order is more complicated. Groups that resort to unconventional participation may threaten the social order and even the government itself. The passage of the Twenty-Sixth Amendment, which lowered the voting age to eighteen, is an example of a government effort to try to channel unconventional participation (strikes and protests) into conventional participation (voting) and thereby maintain order.

Participation and the Models of Democracy

In addition to their role in selecting officeholders, elections also serve to (1) socialize political activity, (2) institutionalize access to political power, and (3) bolster the state's power and authority. Majoritarian participation focuses on elections and emphasizes equality and order. The decentralized

U.S. system of government allows for many forms of participation in addition to voting in elections, and this type of pluralism emphasizes freedom of individuals and groups.

KEY TERMS

terrorism

political participation

conventional participation

unconventional participation

direct action

supportive behavior

influencing behavior

class-action suit

suffrage

franchise

progressivism

direct primary

recall

referendum

initiative

standard socioeconomic model

RESEARCH AND RESOURCES

In addition to the Web resources described at the end of the chapter in your textbook and the selected readings noted at the end of the text, *Congressional Quarterly*'s *Guide to U.S. Elections,* 5th ed. (Washington, D.C.: Congressional Quarterly Press, 2006) offers a gold mine of information for people interested in political parties and elections. Among other things, the volume includes popular vote tallies for:

- The U.S. House of Representatives from 1824 to 2004

- The U.S. Senate from 1913 to 2004 (remember, senators were elected by state legislatures before 1913)

- Governorships from 1789 to 2004

- Presidential primaries from 1912 to 2004

- Southern primaries (a special focus because, in the "solid South," the real political battle has occurred in the primary, not the general election)

Another good source of voting data is the *America Votes* series edited by Alice McGillivray, Rhodes Cool, and Richard Scammon (also published by Congressional Quarterly Press). This handbook provides county-by-county election returns for general elections for president, senator, representative, and governor. It also gives election totals of primary contests for these offices.

Both of these works are great for providing actual election results. However, they do not help you much if you want to investigate some of the issues raised about how people evaluate candidates and how they participate in politics outside the voting booth. To find out more about these issues, you might turn to the end of your textbook for the suggested readings relating to Chapters 4, 5, or 6; but even if you read every book listed, you might not find the specific answer to the exact question that interests you. For example, you might want to know if high-school-educated blacks are as likely as high-school-educated whites to participate in political activities other than voting. You might want to know if women differ from men in their ideological self-placement. Answers to your questions might not be readily available in books, but that does not mean it is impossible to discover the answers.

One way to solve your problem is to find out if computerized survey data are available to you on your campus. The authors of *The Challenge of Democracy* have put together a data set to complement this text. You may want to check with your instructor to see if these materials (called Crosstabs) are available for your use. Your government or political science department may have acquired election surveys provided by the American Political Science Association as part of its SETUPS series. Each SETUPS comes with a student guide that shows how to perform data manipulation. Finally, if your college or university is a member of the Inter-University Consortium for Political and Social Research (ICPSR), it may tap into vast quantities of data from that source. Visit the ICPSR Web site at <http://www.icpsr.umich.edu/>.

GETTING INVOLVED

Voting

The most basic way to participate in U.S. politics is to vote, but as the chapter points out, to vote, you must first be registered. "Motor voter" legislation made the task easier by allowing people to register by simply mailing in a card; in addition, there are some Internet sites available that will help you obtain and fill out the forms needed for registration. You can download forms and instructions from the Federal Election Commission at <http://www.fec.gov/votregis/vr.shtml>. Rock the Vote offers registration forms you can fill out on-line: <http://www.rockthevote.org/>.

Internships

Project Vote Smart, a nonprofit, nonpartisan, grassroots effort, offers internships during the summer and throughout the school year. Interns cover every member of Congress, governors, and the president; they put out national surveys, compile performance evaluations and campaign finance information, work with journalists, and operate a database that supplies voter information. Room and board is provided free at the Great Divide Ranch in Montana. Contact Internship Director, Project Vote Smart, One Common Ground, Philipsburg, Montana 59858. Telephone: (406) 859-8683. E-mail: intern@vote-smart.org. Extensive information on these internships is available on-line at <http://www.vote-smart.org/program_internships.php>.

USING YOUR KNOWLEDGE

1. Using the *Guide to U.S. Elections*, find the election returns for your county for the last three presidential election years. Compare the returns in the presidential races with those in the contests for the House of Representatives. What differences do you notice? Next, compare the House votes in presidential years with those in the intervening, off years. How do the turnout totals compare?

2. Interview a person who has engaged in unconventional participation. Find out what form this unconventional participation took, what the participant's motivation was, and whether he or she felt the activity was successful. What led your interviewee to choose unconventional participation rather than conventional participation?

SAMPLE EXAM QUESTIONS

Multiple-Choice Questions

1. In a democracy, elections are
    a. both necessary and sufficient to guarantee democratic government.
    b. necessary but not sufficient to guarantee democratic government.
    c. sufficient but not necessary to guarantee democratic government.
    d. neither necessary nor sufficient to guarantee democratic government.
2. Which of the following would *least likely* be considered conventional political participation in the United States?
    a. Persuading people to sign a petition
    b. Writing a letter to a public official
    c. Marching in a demonstration
    d. Staging a sit in
3. Which of the following best describes the effectiveness of unconventional participation?
    a. Unconventional participation is never effective.
    b. Unconventional participation is sometimes effective but only if it is peaceful.
    c. Both violent and nonviolent unconventional participation are sometimes effective.
    d. Unconventional participation is the most effective means available to upper-level socioeconomic groups.
4. Gaining government services through "particularized" forms of political participation
    a. serves private interests and may ignore the general will.
    b. is strongly correlated with other forms of participation.
    c. is done mostly by disadvantaged citizens because they have the greatest needs for government aid.
    d. is a typical method of seeking broad benefits for society.
5. Direct political action appeals most to those who
    a. distrust the political system.
    b. have little sense of political efficacy.
    c. are unable to develop a strong sense of group consciousness.
    d. All of the above.
6. Which of the following would *least likely* be considered supportive behavior that expresses allegiance to the country?
    a. Saluting the flag
    b. Voting
    c. Organizing a Fourth of July celebration
    d. Contributing to a particular candidate's campaign
7. Which of the following best describes U.S. political participation in comparison with the activities of citizens in other democracies?
    a. Americans are more likely to vote and participate in lower-initiative activities.
    b. Americans are more likely to participate in all political activities.
    c. Americans are less likely to vote, but they participate at least as much in other participatory activities.
    d. Americans are less likely to participate in unconventional activities.

8. Black females were enfranchised by the
    a.   Fourteenth Amendment.
    b.   Fifteenth Amendment.
    c.   Nineteenth Amendment.
    d.   Twenty-Sixth Amendment.

9. A direct vote by the people on an amendment to a state constitution or on a proposed law is called a(n)
    a.   recall.
    b.   initiative.
    c.   class-action suit.
    d.   referendum.

10. A procedure in which voters propose an issue to be decided by the legislature or by a vote of the people is called
    a.   a recall.
    b.   an initiative.
    c.   suffrage.
    d.   a referendum.

11. Which of the following is most important in predicting conventional political participation in U.S. politics?
    a.   Education
    b.   Race
    c.   Sex
    d.   Region

12. The decline in voter turnout since the 1960s has been associated with all of the following *except*
    a.   lower levels of participation by women.
    b.   lower levels of participation by young people.
    c.   lower levels of party identification.
    d.   the complexity of the registration process.

13. The standard socioeconomic model would predict that
    a.   people with low incomes are most likely to vote.
    b.   older people are more likely to vote.
    c.   women are most likely to resort to unconventional participation.
    d.   white-collar professionals are most likely to participate in politics.

14. The Boston Tea Party and the march from Selma to Montgomery are two examples of
    a.   communist tactics.
    b.   conventional participation.
    c.   unconventional participation.
    d.   institutionalized politics.

15. The passage of the Voting Rights Act of 1965
    a.   gave women the right to vote.
    b.   gave eighteen-year-olds the right to vote.
    c.   suspended discriminatory voting tests and authorized federal supervision of voter registration in the South.
    d.   led to the Selma march.

16. An important measure of the democratic nature of a government is that it
     a. provides adequate opportunities for conventional participation.
     b. leads citizens to choose unconventional modes of participation.
     c. puts an end to all demonstrations.
     d. leads citizens to take direct action to make their voices heard.
17. When the Constitution was first approved, the right to vote was
     a. extended to all white people.
     b. essentially determined by state legislatures.
     c. extended to all property owners.
     d. specifically denied to blacks, women, and those under twenty-one.
18. Progressivism is associated with which of the following?
     a. Direct primaries
     b. Private primaries
     c. White primaries
     d. Integrated primaries
19. A key strategy Martin Luther King, Jr., used in the civil rights movement was
     a. organizing mass letter-writing campaigns to legislators.
     b. direct action to challenge specific cases of discrimination.
     c. holding legislators accountable at the ballot box.
     d. lobbying southern legislators.
20. Which of the following has been linked with lowering voter turnout in the United States?
     a. Cumbersome registration procedures
     b. Holding elections on Tuesdays
     c. Extending the vote to eighteen-year-olds
     d. All of the above

Essay Questions

1. Citizen participation in elections is necessary for a modern representative democracy, but elections themselves are not enough to make a government democratic. Why? Explain the additional forms of political behavior assumed by the pluralist and majoritarian models of democracy.

2. Define political participation and explain the difference between conventional and unconventional participation.

3. Explain why people resort to unconventional political participation. Is it ever effective? Give examples to illustrate your answer.

4. Are Americans politically apathetic? In your answer, compare U.S. political participation with the participation of citizens in other democracies.

5. Write a plan for increasing voter turnout.

ANSWERS TO MULTIPLE-CHOICE QUESTIONS

1. b
2. d
3. c
4. a
5. a
6. d
7. c
8. c
9. d
10. b
11. a
12. a
13. d
14. c
15. c
16. a
17. b
18. a
19. b
20. d

CHAPTER 6

Political Parties, Campaigns, and Elections

LEARNING OBJECTIVES

After reading this chapter you should be able to

- Define the key terms identified in the chapter margins.

- Describe the four most important functions of political parties.

- Trace the history of the major political parties in the United States.

- List the functions performed by minor parties.

- Account for the emergence of a two-party system in the United States.

- Assess the extent of party identification in the United States and its influence on voters' choices.

- Summarize the ideological and organizational differences between Republicans and Democrats.

- Trace the evolution of political campaigning from being party-centered to being candidate-centered.

- Give a thumbnail sketch of the nominating process for Congress, state offices, and the presidency.

- Explain the role and operation of the electoral college.

- Explain how presidential campaigns are currently financed.

- List the three basic strategies used by political campaigns.

- Discuss the role of polling, news coverage, and political advertising in campaigns.

- Describe the operation of long-term and short-term forces on voting choice.

- Decide whether the U.S. system is more pluralist or majoritarian in its operation.

POLITICAL PARTIES, CAMPAIGNS, ELECTIONS, AND THE CHALLENGE OF DEMOCRACY

On the face of it, the U.S. two-party system seems tailor-made for majoritarian democracy. The parties structure the vote into two broad categories and reduce the opportunities for narrowly focused small groups to gain control of the government apparatus. The party system reduces the amount of information voters need to make rational choices. Yet, even this seemingly most majoritarian device does not fully realize its majoritarian potential.

Majority parties are not always able to implement the policies they favor, for example. This inability is partly due to the lack of effective party discipline. That deficiency, in turn, is related to the decentralized structure of American parties. In a sense, the United States has not two but one hundred and two parties—two national organizations and two major parties in each of the fifty states.

On the whole, Democrats and Republicans do differ with respect to their political ideologies. The Democrats are more liberal and tend to place a high value on political and social equality. They are willing to use the government to achieve a more egalitarian economy and society, but they do not wish to use the government to restrict individual freedom (in matters related to lifestyles, reproductive choices, or freedom of expression, for example) to protect the social order. Republicans, on the other hand, are more likely to prefer order and freedom to equality; they prefer limited government when issues of equality are at stake, but they are often willing to use government power to support a particular vision of social order that restricts access to abortion, prohibits homosexual activity, and promotes prayer in public schools.

However, these general statements of the ideological differences between the parties tend to obscure the fact that there are ideological differences within the parties as well. Nonetheless, the difficulties American parties have in maintaining discipline and coordinating the actions of government officials make it hard for them to fulfill the ideals of the majoritarian model. Frustration with the Democratic and Republican parties in 1992 led to widespread popular support for independent candidate Ross Perot in the presidential election and provided the impetus for launching the Reform Party. Although Perot captured 19 percent of the popular vote in 1992, third-party candidates have not enjoyed similar levels of popular support in recent elections. In the highly contentious 2000 election described in the chapter's opening vignette, Green Party nominee Ralph Nader attracted just 2.7 percent of the vote.

Candidates for political office quickly realize that money is the mother's milk of politics. The difficulty for democracy occurs when economic inequality translates into political inequality. Congress began to address the problem by allowing for public financing of presidential campaigns. Presidential candidates whose party performed well in the previous election may accept government money on the condition that they observe certain spending limits as well. This practice promotes political equality. The Bipartisan Campaign Finance Reform Act (BCRA), passed in 2002, created new regulations to govern contributions to candidates. Among other things, BCRA banned soft money contributions to political parties and raised the limit on individual contributions to campaigns. BCRA also linked several contribution limits to inflation, so in future years individuals will be able to contribute more money.

The electoral system itself has features that may make it look rather undemocratic—for example, the electoral college does make it possible for a president to be elected even though he has lost the popular vote. On the other hand, the winner-take-all system in congressional elections appears to be the essence of majoritarianism. Unlike proportional representation systems, it has the effect of leaving minorities without representation. Majoritarians expect that the parties will put forth clear platforms and that their candidates will be held responsible for adhering to them. In practice, these conditions are rarely fulfilled. Instead, we have a system in which candidates rely more on their own efforts than their party's in their campaigns. This self-reliance reduces the relevance of the majoritarian model.

CHAPTER OVERVIEW

Political Parties and Their Functions

A political party is an organization that sponsors candidates for office under the organization's name. The link between political parties and democracy is so close that many democratic theorists believe democracy would be impossible in modern nation-states without parties. Parties perform several important functions in a political system, including the following:

1. *Nominating candidates for election to public office.* This function provides a form of quality control, through peer review by party insiders who know candidates well and judge their acceptability. Parties may also take an active role in recruiting talented candidates for office.

2. *Structuring voting choices.* Parties reduce the number of candidates on a ballot to those that have a realistic chance of winning. This reduces the amount of information voters must acquire to make rational decisions.

3.   *Proposing alternative government programs.* Parties specify general policies their candidates are likely to pursue if elected. These proposed policies usually differ between the parties.

4.   *Coordinating the actions of government officials.* Parties help bridge the separation of powers to produce coordinated policies that are effective in governing the country.

A History of U.S. Party Politics

Today, political parties are institutionalized parts of the U.S. political process. But they were not even mentioned in the Constitution. Although there were opposing factions from the beginning, the first party system began to develop only during the Washington administration. This early system pitted the Federalists against the Democratic Republicans. By the 1820s, the Democratic Republicans so dominated this system that the Federalists did not even field a candidate. Soon, factionalism developed within the Democratic Republican party, which split in two, with one wing becoming the Democratic party. The year 1854 saw the formation of a new party opposed to the spread of slavery, the Republican party.

Thus, the election of 1856 marked the first contests between Democrats and Republicans, the parties constituting our present-day party system. Since then, there have been three critical elections signaling new, enduring electoral realignments in which one or the other of the two parties became dominant. In the period from 1860 to 1894, there was a rough balance between the parties, followed by a period of Republican dominance from the critical election of 1896 until 1930. The critical election of 1932 produced a Democratic majority, which persisted largely unbroken until 1994, when the Republicans gained control of both houses of Congress. We may currently be in a period of electoral dealignment, in which party loyalties are less important to voters.

The American Two-Party System

The history of U.S. party politics has been dominated by successive two-party systems, but minor parties—including bolter parties, farm-labor parties, ideological protest parties, and single-issue parties—have made special contributions to U.S. politics. Although third parties have not generally fared well as vote getters, they have helped people express discontent with the choices offered by the dominant parties. Third parties function as policy advocates and as safety valves for the system.

The persistence of the two-party system in the United States is aided by the country's election rules. In almost all U.S. elections, single winners are chosen by a simple plurality of votes within a geographic district. A presidential candidate wins election by amassing a majority of electoral votes across the country. The federal structure itself also contributes to the staying power of the Democrats and Republicans. Even when one party wins a landslide presidential election, the losing party is still likely to retain significant strength in many individual states. This makes it possible for the minority party to rebuild.

The longevity of the present two-party system is also a result of the tendency for citizens to be socialized from childhood to think of themselves as Democrats or Republicans. They identify with one or the other party, and this identification predisposes them to vote for candidates of that party. Whereas a citizen's actual voting behavior may change from election to election or from candidate to candidate, party identification changes more slowly over time, as citizens who vote against their party gradually reassess their identification.

Party Ideology and Organization

The Democratic and Republican parties are both capitalist parties, but they differ in their ideological orientations. In 2004, Republicans fit into the conservative camp, while Democrats stressed equality. Republicans choose limited government where issues of equality and redistribution of wealth are concerned, but they are willing to use the government to promote their own values of social order. Democrats, in contrast, will commit themselves to an activist government that promotes equality but would restrict the government from interfering with people's freedom to define their own lifestyle.

The federal structure is apparent in the organization of the country's political parties. Each party has separate state and national organizations. At the national level, each party has a national convention, national committee, congressional party conference, and congressional campaign committee. Historically, the role of the national organizations was fairly limited, but in the 1970s, Democratic procedural reforms and Republican organizational reforms increased the activity of the national organizations. The national organizations have increased in strength and financial resources, yet state party organizations are still essentially independent in organizing their state activities, and so the system remains decentralized.

The Model of Responsible Party Government

Responsible parties are a key feature of majoritarian theory. For a party system to work, the following four factors are necessary: (1) the parties must present clear, coherent programs; (2) the voters must choose candidates on the basis of these programs; (3) the winning party must carry out its program; and (4) the voters must hold the incumbents responsible for their program at the next election.

Parties and Candidates

Election campaigns, or organized efforts to persuade voters to choose one candidate over the others, have changed considerably over the years. In general, political parties play a much smaller role than they once did. The parties supply a label, as well as services and some funds. Candidates must campaign for their party's nomination as well as for election. In the age of electronic media, campaigns have become more candidate-centered than party-centered.

Unlike most other political parties in the world, U.S. political parties now usually nominate their candidates through election by party voters. For most state and local offices, candidates are chosen through primary elections of various types—*open, closed, modified open,* and *modified closed.* Candidates for the presidency are chosen at national party nominating conventions. Most convention delegates are now selected in party primaries or caucuses before the convention is held. As a result, in recent years, the outcome of the nominating conventions has been known long beforehand. The Iowa caucus and New Hampshire primary have become early tests of potential candidates' appeal to party regulars and to ordinary voters. The nominating process today tends to favor candidates who appeal to party identifiers, but the candidates who win nomination must rely on their own organization and resources rather than on the national party.

Elections

Presidents are elected indirectly by the electoral college. Each state's number of electoral votes is equal to the size of its congressional delegation (senators plus representatives). The District of Columbia also has three votes in the electoral college. Though the winner of the popular election can lose in the electoral college as Al Gore did in 2000, this has rarely occurred. In most states, electoral votes are awarded on a winner-take-all basis. Candidates for Congress are elected in a first-past-the-post system, which tends to magnify the victory margins of the winning party.

Campaigns

Candidates must pay attention to the political context of each election. It matters whether the candidate is a challenger or an incumbent. The size of the district, its voting population, and its socioeconomic makeup are also important.

Although good candidates and a strong organization are valuable resources in modern political campaigning, money is central. In recent years Congress has moved to set strict reporting requirements for campaign contributions and created the Federal Election Commission to monitor campaign finances. Presidential nominees are eligible for public funds to support their campaigns if they agree to spend only those funds. Wealthy candidates can spend their own money without limit, but contributions to candidates from outside sources are tightly controlled.

Campaign strategies may be party-centered, issue-oriented, or image-oriented. Candidates use a mix of polls and focus groups to design their strategies. Most campaigns emphasize using the media in two ways: through news coverage and political advertising. Each of these approaches to the media seeks the same primary goal: candidate name recognition. News coverage is often limited to brief sound bites, however. Candidates have successfully turned to new venues to boost their name recognition, including the purchase of "infomercials" on television, appearances on MTV, and more recently, using the Internet as a low-cost fundraising tool.

Explaining Voting Choice

Voting decisions are related to both long- and short-term factors. Among long-term factors, party identification is still the most important. Candidate attributes and policy positions are both important short-term factors. Although issues still do not play the most important role in voting choices, research suggests that there is now closer alignment between voters' issue positions and their party identification. Given the importance of long-term factors in shaping voting choice, the influence of campaigns is limited. But in close elections, a swing of only a few votes may change the outcome, and so the campaign assumes greater importance.

Campaigns, Elections, and Parties

As candidates rely more on the media, U.S. election campaigns have become highly personalized, and party organizations have waned in importance. In evaluating U.S. parties according to their performance as instruments of responsible government (the majoritarian model), we find that they do present distinctive programs and do tend to pursue their announced policies when in office. However, voters do not choose between candidates according to party programs. And finally, voters do not hold the party accountable for implementing its program. For these reasons, the operation of U.S. parties more closely resembles the pluralist model, with the parties acting as two huge interest groups.

KEY TERMS

political party

nomination

political system

critical election

electoral realignment

electoral dealignment

two-party system

majority representation

proportional representation

party identification

party platform

national convention

national committee

party conference

congressional campaign committee

party machine

responsible party government

election campaign

primary election

closed primary

open primary

modified closed primary

modified open primary

presidential primary

caucus/convention

front-loading

general election

straight ticket

split ticket

first-past-the-post election

open election

Federal Election Commission (FEC)

hard money

Bipartisan Campaign Finance Reform Act (BCRA)

soft money

527 committee

RESEARCH AND RESOURCES

1. This chapter indicates that the U.S. system is built on a loose confederation of independent state-party organizations rather than a rigidly hierarchical structure with a national party at its apex. Indeed, until recently, the national party all but went out of existence in nonpresidential election years. Thus, the two most conspicuous products of national party organizations have been the presidential nominating conventions and the party platforms.

    A good online directory of major and minor U.S. political parties is <http://www.politics1.com/parties.htm>. For the text of party platforms since 1840, try <http://www.americanpresidency.org>. For information on parties throughout the world, see <http://www.politicalresources.net/>.

2. Because money is so important to political campaigning, you might want to know where candidates get their money. One good source is Barbara Rogers' *The Almanac of Federal PACS*

2004-2005 (Washington, D.C.: Congressional Quarterly Press, 2004). This work provides detailed data on PAC revenue and contributions, along with tables listing all receipts, revenues, and ending balances for every member of Congress.

For up-to-date information delivered electronically, go to the Federal Election Commission's Web site at <http://www.fec.gov>. The FEC provides a wealth of data on candidates' receipts and expenditures, as well as information about PAC contributions. Finally, the Internet exercises in your textbook point you towards <www.colorofmoney.org>, a remarkable online resource showing who is giving what to whom in your own neighborhood and across the nation.

USING YOUR KNOWLEDGE

1. Find and read the Democratic and Republican platforms for an election held within the last ten years. Note the areas of similarity and difference between the two. In the election year you chose to examine, would you say that observers who claim, "there's not a dime's worth of difference between the two parties" were correct? Give evidence to support your answer.

2. Use an online resource to find out where your own senators' or representatives' campaign funds came from. What proportion came from PACs? What kind of PACs provided the largest share of funds? Is your senator or representative on any committees that handle issues related to the contributing PACs' areas of concern? How much money did the defeated candidate receive from PACs in the last election?

GETTING INVOLVED

If you are interested in working for a political party, you may want to begin by contacting the local party organization in your county or by joining the Young Democrats or Young Republicans on your campus. Each party has its own congressional campaign Web sites. You can find the Republican sites at <http://www.nrcc.org> and <http://www.nrsc.org>; the Democratic sites are at <http://www.dccc.org> and <http://www.dscc.org>. Some internships are available for students who would like to become involved with the parties on the national level. Contact information for these committees is available on their websites. Interns working for these committees might conduct research, assist in fund-raising, work with communications, and tend to mail and administrative details.

SAMPLE EXAM QUESTIONS

Multiple-Choice Questions

1. One way that parties differ from interest groups is that parties
    a.   contribute funds to candidates.
    b.   sponsor candidates for office as their avowed representative.
    c.   represent identifiable interests.
    d.   mobilize get-out-the-vote campaigns.
2. A critical election is one in which
    a.   an incumbent president is defeated.
    b.   an electoral realignment occurs.
    c.   divided government is produced.
    d.   divided government is ended.

3. Which of the following is not considered to have been a critical election?

   a. 1860
   b. 1896
   c. 1920
   d. 1932

4. The Democratic coalition under Franklin Roosevelt included all of the following *except*

   a. southern whites.
   b. northern Protestant businessmen.
   c. Jews.
   d. Catholics.

5. The Prohibition Party is an example of a

   a. bolter party.
   b. single-issue party.
   c. farmer-labor party.
   d. party of ideological protest.

6. Minor parties often contribute to the political process by

   a. transforming themselves into major parties.
   b. acting as safety valves, which allows their followers to express their discontent.
   c. getting enough votes to change electoral outcomes.
   d. getting enough votes to win elections.

7. An example of a party of ideological protest is the

   a. Libertarian Party.
   b. Prohibitionist Party.
   c. Progressive Party.
   d. Free-Soil Party.

8. Which of the following characterizes the platforms of the Democrats and Republicans?

   a. Both are essentially capitalist parties.
   b. The Republicans are capitalist, but the Democrats are not.
   c. The Republicans pledge themselves to equality, whereas the Democrats support freedom.
   d. The Republicans pledge themselves to limit all spheres of government activity, whereas the Democrats pledge themselves to increase all spheres of government activity.

9. Imagine an election in which ten legislative seats are at stake. Party A receives 60 percent of the votes cast. Party B gets 30 percent of the votes. Party C tallies 10 percent of the votes. As a result, Party A is awarded six seats; Party B, three seats; and Party C, one seat. This is an example of a(n)

   a. proportional representation system.
   b. majority representation system.
   c. electoral dealignment.
   d. first-past-the-post electoral system.

10. The most distinguishing feature of U.S. political parties is their

   a. tight party discipline.
   b. clear ideological definition.
   c. hierarchical organization.
   d. absence of centralized power.

11. In the 1970s, the national parties expanded their activities by

   a. introducing organizational or procedural reforms.
   b. exerting direct control over national, state, and local campaigns.
   c. assuming the main fund-raising responsibility for party candidates.
   d. all of the above.

12. Party identification is

    a.   a measure of how well voters recognize the names of major parties.
    b.   part of the credentials check at national conventions.
    c.   a measure of a voter's sense of psychological attachment to a party.
    d.   a measure of how well voters match a party with its candidates.

13. Unlike today, in the early 1950s, most white southerners belonged to

    a.   the Republican party.
    b.   the Democratic party.
    c.   the Prohibition Party.
    d.   None of the above.

14. As far as political parties are concerned, the Constitution

    a.   limits the number of major parties to two but allows an unlimited number of minor parties.
    b.   limits the number of major parties to two and allows no more than ten minor parties.
    c.   says nothing.
    d.   provides that they be organized at the state level.

15. The model of responsible party government includes all of the following principles *except* that

    a.   parties should present clear and coherent programs to voters.
    b.   voters should choose candidates according to their ability to carry out their goals.
    c.   the winning party should carry out its program once in office.
    d.   voters should hold the governing party responsible at the next election for executing its program.

16. In the contemporary U.S. political campaign,

    a.   parties play the central role.
    b.   parties play a larger role than they did in the 1950s.
    c.   parties provide candidates with most of their information about public opinion.
    d.   candidates rather than parties have assumed center stage.

17. Which of the following describes how candidates for Congress are usually nominated today?

    a.   By party activists at conventions
    b.   By party voters in primaries
    c.   By all voters in primaries
    d.   None of the above

18. Primary elections that allow voters to decide at their respective polling places whether to take a Republican or a Democratic ballot are called

    a.   direct primaries.
    b.   closed primaries.
    c.   open primaries.
    d.   presidential primaries.

19. Rules for selecting delegates to national party conventions

    a.   are uniform throughout the nation.
    b.   vary from state to state but not from party to party.
    c.   vary from party to party but not from state to state.
    d.   vary both from state to state and from party to party.

20. The first major tests of a presidential candidate's appeal occur in

    a.   Iowa and Vermont.
    b.   Vermont and New Hampshire.
    c.   Connecticut and Missouri.
    d.   Iowa and New Hampshire.

21. Which of these scenarios best characterizes the presidential nominating process today?

     a.   Party-dominated, many primaries, long campaigns
     b.   Candidate-dominated, many primaries, long campaigns
     c.   Candidate-dominated, few primaries, short campaigns
     d.   Party-dominated, few primaries, short campaigns

22. Most modern candidates who win a party presidential nomination do so

     a.   because their party's leaders have selected them.
     b.   in spite of the preferences of most of the people who identify with their party.
     c.   on their own, without help from their national party organization.
     d.   because the nominating process rarely attracts more than one plausible candidate.

23. An argument frequently made in favor of the electoral college system is that

     a.   it preserves an emphasis on federalism as embodied in the Constitution.
     b.   it promotes majority rule.
     c.   due to electoral reforms and population changes, it is no longer possible for a candidate with a minority of popular votes to win the electoral vote.
     d.   All of the above.

24. In the general election, presidential campaigns

     a.   must be privately financed to hold down the federal deficit.
     b.   must be entirely publicly financed under law.
     c.   may receive public funds if they agree to accept and spend only those funds.
     d.   must act to limit other groups wishing to promote their candidate.

25. Which of the following has resulted from public funding on campaign financing?

     a.   Increased campaign costs
     b.   Greater equality in spending among candidates
     c.   Less candidate attention to small contributors
     d.   More party control of the process

26. An electoral strategy that stresses the candidate's experience and leadership ability would probably be considered

     a.   party-centered.
     b.   issue-oriented.
     c.   image-oriented.
     d.   negative campaigning.

27. Which of the following is the first objective of paid advertising?

     a.   Name recognition
     b.   Awareness of a candidate's good qualities
     c.   Awareness of an opponent's negative qualities
     d.   Awareness of issue positions

28. When a voter selects candidates from different parties for different offices, the voter is said to vote a(n)

     a.   split ticket.
     b.   nonpartisan ticket.
     c.   party-oriented ticket.
     d.   open ticket.

29. An effect of ticket splitting has been

     a.   that candidates with a minority of electoral votes may reach the White House.
     b.   that candidates with a popular majority may lose their races.
     c.   divided government.
     d.   a move toward more closed primaries.

30. The most important long-term force affecting U.S. elections is
    a. party identification.
    b. candidate attributes.
    c. candidate issue positions.
    d. race.

Essay Questions

1. The history of the U.S. party system has been a tale of two-party dominance. Nevertheless, third parties have often served special functions. Describe those functions, and give specific examples.

2. Why has the two-party system dominated U.S. politics?

3. Is there "a dime's worth of difference" between Democrats and Republicans? Support your answer with concrete illustrations focusing on party ideologies and organization.

4. Discuss the functions that parties perform for the U.S. political system.

5. Outline the ways today's campaigns for a party's presidential nomination differ from those of the first half of the century.

6. How does the effort to regulate campaign finances raise the tension between freedom and equality?

7. Explain how the electoral college fits into the electoral process. Should it be abolished? Present the main arguments on each side of the issue. Which side do you find most compelling? Why?

8. Explain the most important short- and long-term factors affecting voting choice in the United States.

ANSWERS TO MULTIPLE-CHOICE QUESTIONS

1. b
2. b
3. c
4. b
5. b
6. b
7. a
8. a
9. a
10. d
11. a
12. c
13. b
14. c
15. b
16. d
17. b
18. c
19. d
20. d
21. b
22. c
23. a
24. c
25. b
26. c
27. a
28. a
29. c
30. a

CHAPTER 7

Interest Groups

LEARNING OBJECTIVES

After reading this chapter you should be able to

- Define the key terms identified in the chapter margins.

- Outline the positive and negative roles played by interest groups in U.S. politics.

- Explain how interest groups form.

- Create a profile of the kind of person most likely to be represented by an interest group.

- Describe the major resources that interest groups use to influence policy.

- List the tactics used by interest groups to win the support of policymakers.

- Account for the recent increase in the number of interest groups.

- Discuss the impact of high-tech lobbying by interest groups.

INTEREST GROUPS AND THE CHALLENGE OF DEMOCRACY

Following the September 11, 2001, attacks on the United States, the U.S. government was besieged by lobbyists offering advice or products to help in the war against terrorism. As the opening vignette explains, it is not easy to draw a clear distinction between lobbies we find virtuous and lobbies we find selfish. All interest groups are part of pluralist democracy.

The founders anticipated that factions or interest groups would play an important part in politics. James Madison's writings show that they believed factions would thrive in an atmosphere of freedom: "Liberty is to faction what air is to fire." The only way to eliminate factions or interest-group politics was to curtail freedom. The founders were certainly not prepared to abandon the very value for which they had fought the Revolutionary War. So they proposed using factions to combat factions, with the government serving as the mediator.

More recently, pluralist political scientists have resurrected these Madisonian hopes. They have made it clear that U.S. politics is not majoritarian but has interest groups at its center. They also expect interests to counterbalance one another and for the system to provide open access. However, as this chapter indicates, some interests, notably those of business, are much better represented than others. Opportunities for access may often depend on money. The fact that there are no "poor PACs" or no "food stamp PACs" suggests that the interests of the poor may not be adequately represented. Insofar as political equality means "one person, one vote," Americans are pretty much equal; but if political equality means more than that, then it follows that where contemporary interest-group politics are concerned, social inequality leads to political inequality.

So why not limit the activities of interest groups to promote open access and make pluralism function as Madison expected it would? The answer is that limiting interest groups also means limiting the right of the people to petition their government—a fundamental freedom guaranteed under the Constitution.

CHAPTER OVERVIEW

Interest Groups and the American Political Tradition

Interest groups, or lobbies—organized bodies of individuals who share some political goals and try to influence policy decisions—have always been a part of U.S. politics. The Constitution itself was designed to preserve freedom by relying on what we now call pluralist politics, or, in Madisonian terms, the use of factions to counteract other factions. But giving people freedom to organize does not necessarily promote political equality. Thus, the value people place on equality may determine whether they believe that interest groups are bad or good.

Interest groups perform various important functions in the U.S. system: they represent their members to the government; they provide channels for citizen participation; they educate their members, government officials, and the public at large; they build the public agenda by putting issues before the government; and they monitor programs important to their members.

How Interest Groups Form

Modern pluralists believe that interest groups further democracy. They believe interest groups form naturally by a process similar to the "invisible hand" in economics. When unorganized people are adversely affected by change, they organize themselves into groups to protect their interests. Yet, empirical evidence suggests that this doesn't always happen—more than a simple disturbance is required. Strong leadership—provided by interest-group entrepreneurs—may be critically important in forming an interest group; in addition, social class is also a factor in interest-group formation. Although the poor and less educated do form groups to advance their interests, middle- and upper-class individuals are much more likely to see the value of interest groups and to organize.

Interest Group Resources

An interest group's strength and effectiveness usually depend on its resources. These resources include members, lobbyists, and money. Interest groups work hard to build their memberships and to combat the "free rider" problem. They also keep their members well informed of group activities. Lobbyists, preferably Washington insiders with previous government experience, present the group's views to legislators and officials of the executive branch. Currently, an important resource used by interest groups is the political action committee (PAC). This type of organization enables a group to make political campaign contributions more easily, in the hope of obtaining better access to officials. PACs may make influence a function of money (thereby reducing political equality), but limiting PACs would amount to a restriction on freedom of expression. Furthermore, PACs also allow small givers to pool their resources to obtain more clout.

Lobbying Tactics

Interest groups may seek help from the legislature, the courts, or the administration. Lobbyists carry out their task in several ways. They may use direct lobbying aimed at policymakers themselves—through legal advocacy, personal presentations, or committee testimony. Alternatively, they may rely on grassroots lobbying by enlisting group members to pressure elected officials through letters or political protests. Lobbyists may also use information campaigns, bringing their views to the attention of the general public through public relations methods. These campaigns may involve publicizing the voting records of legislators or sponsoring research. Lobbyists also use e-mail and the Internet as tools of the trade. Finally, lobbyists may lobby together through coalition building.

Is the System Biased?

Are the decisions made in a pluralist system fair? Perhaps, if all significant interests are represented by lobbying groups and the government listens to the views of all major interests as it makes policy. Yet, research shows that interest groups have a membership bias—some parts of society are better organized than others. But in addition to groups motivated by the self-interest of their members, there are also citizen groups motivated for reasons other than economic self-interest; these groups seek to achieve a common good that benefits all citizens. Initially, most of these groups were liberal. More recently, there has been growth in conservative citizen groups working on behalf of causes such as the right-to-life movement or "family values." The success of liberal groups in the 1960s and 1970s led businesses to increase their lobbying efforts. Since corporations have considerable resources, they may be better equipped to gain power than are public interest lobbies, which rely on voluntary private contributions.

Although the First Amendment guarantees the right to organize as a central part of U.S. politics, interest groups may confer unacceptable advantages on some segments of the community. Thus, some efforts have been made to limit their impact, through federal regulation of lobbying, disclosure laws, gift bans, and public financing of presidential campaigns.

KEY TERMS

interest group

lobbyist

agenda building

program monitoring

interest group entrepreneur

free rider problem

trade association

political action committee (PAC)

direct lobbying

grassroots lobbying

information campaign

coalition building

membership bias

citizen group

RESEARCH AND RESOURCES

One of the most significant recent developments in U.S. politics has been the proliferation of PACs. Several useful reference works on interest groups and PACs are available. In addition to the selected readings and Web resources described at the end of the chapter in your textbook, a particularly valuable publication is Barbara Rogers' *The Almanac of Federal PACs*: 2004-2005 (Washington, D.C.: Congressional Quarterly Press, 2004). Provides up-to-date descriptions of the interests and orientations of individual PACs, along with a record of their recent giving activities.

Some college libraries subscribe to the Gale Research Company's *Associations Unlimited* online database, which gives membership and budget statistics for thousands of organizations. Gale Research

Company also publishes a print directory, *The Encyclopedia of Associations* (Detroit: Gale Research Company, 2005), containing information on over 22,000 organizations.

For online information about PAC contributions, try the Federal Election Commission website at <http://www.fec.gov/>. Curious who is behind BAC PAC, BLOCKPAC, or BIRDPAC? Among other invaluable resources on the FEC site is a directory deciphering PACronyms, the often confusing acronyms, initials, and common names of political action committees involved in federal elections. See <http://www.fec.gov/pubrec/pacronyms/pacronyms.shtml>.

Some lobbying firms describe the services they offer. For a list, try <http://dir.yahoo.com/Business_and_Economy/Business_to_Business/Government/Lobbying/>.

USING YOUR KNOWLEDGE

Search the FEC Web site for one of the senators or representatives elected to represent your district in 2004 (or look up your most or least favorite member of Congress) using the search form at <http://herndon1.sdrdc.com/fecimg/norcansea.html>. After you have found a listing for the candidate, look for an option to view "committees who gave to this candidate." How much money did this member of Congress receive from PACs? Which PACs contributed? How did the contributions from PACs compare to the contributions from the candidate's national party organization? How did the winner's PAC contributions compare to those received by the losing candidate?

GETTING INVOLVED

Opportunities abound to learn more about the Washington community and the think tanks and lobbyists that play such an important role in policymaking. The list provided here will give you some idea of the range of possibilities available.

Internships at Think Tanks

The American Enterprise Institute (AEI) assigns interns to resident scholars working in economic policy, foreign and defense policy, or social and political policy. Internships are available in the fall, spring, or summer and run twelve weeks. They are unpaid. Deadlines are September 15 for fall, December 1 for spring, and April 1 for summer. For further information, contact the American Enterprise Institute, Intern Coordinator, 1150 Seventeenth St., NW, Washington, D.C. 20036. Telephone: (202) 862-7166. Online site: <http://www.aei.org/job/intern.htm>. E-mail: internships@aei.org.

The Brookings Institution assigns its unpaid interns to work on research involving political institutions, processes, and policies. Internships are available in program areas such as governance studies, foreign policy studies, economic studies, and metropolitan policy. Deadlines are generally June 1 for fall, October 15 for spring, and February 15 for summer, although the Brookings website occasionally lists immediate openings. Write to the Brookings Institution, Internship Coordinator, 1775 Massachusetts Ave., NW, Washington, D.C. 20036. Online site: <http://www.brookings.edu/admin/internships.htm>.

Common Cause uses interns to work for grassroots lobbying efforts as well as to monitor congressional meetings and perform other research. Interns should be prepared to commit two days a week to this volunteer internship. The deadline to apply for summer internships is mid-March. To apply, send a resumè and cover letter to internships@commoncause.org. For further information, contact Common Cause, Volunteer Office, 1250 Connecticut Ave., NW, Suite 600, Washington, D.C. 20036-2613. Telephone: (202) 833-1200. Online site: <http://www.commoncause.org/>.

Internships with Interest Groups

The Feminist Majority Foundation offers the chance to lobby for women's issues, including reproductive rights, sexual harassment, and women's rights. Internships are two months long and unpaid. Student interns may work in the D.C. or Los Angeles offices. For more information, write to Feminist Majority Foundation, 1600 Wilson Boulevard, Suite 801, Arlington, VA 22209, phone: (703) 522-2214, toll-free: (866) 444-3652, fax: (703) 522-2219, or 433 S. Beverly Drive, Beverly Hills, CA 90212, phone: (310) 556-2500, fax: (310) 556-2509. Online site: <http://www.feminist.org/intern/>.

Americans for Democratic Action, long the nation's best-known liberal organization, offers full- and part-time internships during the school year; there is no pay, but hours are flexible, and arrangements may be made with home institutions to coordinate course credit. For further information, contact Americans for Democratic Action, 1625 K Street, Suite 210, Washington, D.C. 20006. Telephone: (202) 785-5980. Online site: <http://www.adaction.org/>.

The Union of Concerned Scientists involves students in research and lobbying on issues related to arms control and the impact of technology. The internships are paid, and thirty to forty hours of work per week is the normal expectation. For further information, contact the Union of Concerned Scientists, 1616 P Street, NW, Suite 310, Washington, D.C. 20036. Telephone: (202) 332-0900. Online site: <http://www.ucsusa.org/>.

The National Taxpayers Union works for lower taxes and reduced government spending. It offers paid internships to students interested in working on researching taxpayer issues; preparing a congressional spending analysis; and lobbying at the grassroots, national, and state levels. Students should apply six weeks ahead of the desired starting date and by April 1 for summer internships. For further information, contact the Internship Program, National Taxpayers Union, 108 N. Alfred Street, Alexandria, VA 22314. Telephone: (703) 683-5700. Online site: <http://www.ntu.org>.

SAMPLE EXAM QUESTIONS

Multiple-Choice Questions

1. The proliferation of interest groups in U.S. politics
   a. serves to promote political equality.
   b. was opposed by James Madison.
   c. fits well with the majoritarian model of democracy.
   d. is a result of a commitment to freedom.
2. According to Alexis de Tocqueville, the number of organizations in the United States indicates a
   a. perverse and greedy culture.
   b. lack of skill in government.
   c. strong democratic culture.
   d. weak democratic culture.
3. The idea that interest groups originate when unorganized people are adversely affected by change
   a. is called the disturbance theory.
   b. was proven by the experience of people living in the West End of Boston.
   c. is a rejection of pluralist theory.
   d. is a realist view of interest group formation.
4. The development of the United Farm Workers Union is a good example of
   a. the invisible-hand theory of interest group formation.
   b. the importance of interest group leadership.
   c. the relationship of social class to interest group formation.
   d. All of the above.

5.   Which of the following is an example of a citizen group?

   a.   The Business Roundtable
   b.   The American Medical Association
   c.   The AFL-CIO
   d.   The Children's Defense Fund

6.   Interest groups sometimes have trouble attracting members when people are able to benefit from the group's activities without having to contribute to its support. This difficulty is called the

   a.   "free rider" problem.
   b.   disturbance theory.
   c.   laissez-faire problem.
   d.   invisible-hand problem.

7.   Political action committees

   a.   have no limits on the money they may contribute to candidates.
   b.   rarely reflect the interests of ideological groups.
   c.   are a method of using money to gain access to public officials.
   d.   promote political equality.

8.   Most PAC contributions

   a.   are given based upon pragmatic strategies.
   b.   are given to challengers to oust incumbents.
   c.   are given based upon ideological strategies.
   d.   are given by citizen groups.

9.   The most commonly used direct lobbying tactic is

   a.   the personal presentation of a group's position.
   b.   the letter-writing campaign.
   c.   testifying at committee hearings.
   d.   legal advocacy.

10. Who would be most likely to belong to a group working to advance their interests?

   a.   People receiving veterans' benefits
   b.   Welfare recipients
   c.   Food stamp recipients
   d.   People receiving Medicaid

11. Coalitions formed for lobbying purposes

   a.   tend to be informal, ad hoc arrangements.
   b.   usually waste resources.
   c.   are prohibited under federal law.
   d.   generally center around long-term goals and broad issue areas.

12. A major difference between citizen groups and other lobbies is that citizen groups

   a.   do not generally pursue the economic self-interests of their members.
   b.   are always poorly funded.
   c.   do not support conservative causes.
   d.   still rely primarily on grassroots tactics.

13. The text argues that high-tech lobbying techniques

   a.   have replaced old-fashioned letter-writing campaigns.
   b.   work to the advantage of those already well represented.
   c.   by democratizing access, work to make U.S. politics more majoritarian.
   d.   All of the above.

14. All of the following contributed to the increase of business lobbies in Washington *except* the
    a. expanded scope of federal government activity.
    b. success of liberal public interest groups.
    c. success of interest groups on the religious right.
    d. All of the above have contributed to the increase of business lobbies.

15. As the U.S. system becomes increasingly centered around interest group advocacy,
    a. majoritarian democracy is enhanced.
    b. political parties are strengthened.
    c. business has an advantage.
    d. interest groups control the party nominating functions.

16. Which of these is *not* a tactic commonly used in direct lobbying?
    a. Meeting with members of Congress
    b. Meeting with congressional staff
    c. Testifying at congressional hearings
    d. Direct mail campaigns

17. According to James Madison, interest groups were
    a. natural, but their effects could be controlled.
    b. unnatural and could be eliminated.
    c. natural but could be eliminated by establishing democratic institutions.
    d. unnatural and would never form in the United States.

18. According to the text, lobbyists
    a. are poorly paid.
    b. have often had previous government service.
    c. must be lawyers.
    d. rely mainly on arm-twisting and backslapping to get their way.

19. The largest segment of the interest group universe is made up of
    a. citizen groups.
    b. business groups.
    c. unions.
    d. professional associations.

20. The disturbance theory asserts that
    a. when individuals are threatened, they band together and form interest groups.
    b. government regulation is necessary to promote interest group competition.
    c. protest demonstrations are the most effective way for groups to promote their positions.
    d. interest group entrepreneurs should organize protests and other disruptions.

Essay Questions

1. What benefits do interest groups provide to the U.S. political system?

2. Describe the key variables that explain interest group success. Give examples to justify your choices.

3. Explain the "free rider" problem.

4. How has the growth of interest group activity in Washington affected the tension between pluralism and majoritarianism?

5. "On the whole, PACs are detrimental to democracy." Evaluate this statement by outlining the pros and cons of PACs and explaining the reasons why you agree or disagree with it.

ANSWERS TO MULTIPLE-CHOICE QUESTIONS

1. d
2. c
3. a
4. b
5. d
6. a
7. c
8. a
9. a
10. a
11. a
12. a
13. b
14. c
15. c
16. d
17. a
18. b
19. b
20. a

CHAPTER 8

Congress

LEARNING OBJECTIVES

After reading this chapter you should be able to

- Define the key terms identified in the chapter margins.

- Outline the constitutional duties of the House and Senate.

- Account for the "incumbency effect."

- Describe the background characteristics of a typical member of Congress.

- Sketch the process by which a bill becomes a law.

- Explain the importance of the committee system in the legislative process.

- Distinguish between congressional rules of procedure and norms of behavior.

- Discuss how the modern filibuster differs from the classic filibuster.

- Explain the dilemma representatives face in choosing between trustee and delegate roles.

- Evaluate the extent to which the structure of Congress promotes pluralist or majoritarian politics.

CONGRESS AND THE CHALLENGE OF DEMOCRACY

The structure of Congress, both as designed by the founders and as it has evolved over the past two centuries, heightens the tension between pluralism and majoritarianism in U.S. politics. Under the Constitution, the system of checks and balances divides complete lawmaking power between Congress and the president. In addition, under the Constitution, members of Congress are elected from particular states or congressional districts and ultimately depend on the voters from those constituencies to re-elect them. Two facts suggest majoritarian influences on Congress. First, to become law, legislation must ultimately be passed by a majority vote in each house. Second, in recent years at least, the party system, which may act as a majoritarian influence on politics, has had a greater impact on the way members actually vote.

Much about the structure of Congress reinforces pluralism. The committee structure encourages members of Congress to gain expertise in narrow policy areas. The experience that members gain in these areas often leads them to look after particular constituencies or special interests. Furthermore, because the outcome of the legislative process is usually the result of vote trading, logrolling, bargaining, and coalition building, any final product is likely to represent all sorts of concessions to various interests.

CHAPTER OVERVIEW

The Origin and Powers of Congress

The U.S. Congress is a bicameral (two-house) legislature. Its basic structure grew out of the Great Compromise at the Constitutional Convention. As a result of that compromise, each state is represented in the upper house (or Senate) by two senators, who serve staggered six-year terms; in the lower house (the House of Representatives), states are represented according to their population. Members of the lower house serve two-year terms. In 1929, the total number of representatives was fixed at 435. Whenever the population shifts (as demonstrated by a decennial census), the country's 435 single-member legislative districts must be reapportioned to reflect the changes and provide equal representation.

Congress makes laws. For a bill to become a law, both the House and the Senate must pass it in the same form. The two legislative chambers differ in some of their duties and powers. All revenue bills must originate in the House; the House has the power to impeach officials. The Senate tries cases of impeachment; that body also approves treaties and major presidential appointments.

Electing Members of Congress

Although elections offer voters the opportunity to express their approval or disapproval of congressional performance, voters rarely reject House incumbents. Polls show that the public lacks confidence in Congress as a whole and supports term limits; on the other hand, most people are satisfied with their own particular legislator. Incumbents have enormous advantages that help them keep their seats. For example, incumbents are generally much more attractive to PACs and find it easier to obtain funds for re-election campaigns. Incumbents usually have greater name recognition; they acquire this name recognition by using free mailing privileges and by building a reputation for handling casework. Gerrymandering during redistricting may also work to the benefit of an incumbent. Senate races tend to be more competitive than House races; incumbency is less of an advantage in the Senate, partly because of the greater visibility of challengers in Senate races. When challengers do defeat incumbents, it is often the case that the previous election was close or the ideology and party identification of the state's voters favors the challenger.

The people who make up the U.S. Congress tend to be white, male professionals with college or graduate degrees. Women and minority-group members are relatively few in Congress. To remedy this situation, some people favor descriptive representation; others argue that devices such as racial gerrymandering discriminate unjustly against white candidates. Recent court decisions such as *Shaw* v. *Reno* have dealt setbacks to racial gerrymandering, but the Supreme Court has indicated that race may be taken into account when drawing congressional boundaries as long as it is not the "dominant and controlling" factor.

How Issues Get on the Congressional Agenda

Although many issues on the congressional agenda seem to be perennial, new issues do emerge. Sometimes, a crisis or visible event such as the September 11 hijackings prompts Congress to act; at other times, congressional champions of particular proposals are able to win powerful supporters for their ideas. Congressional leaders and committee chairpersons also have the power to place items on the congressional agenda; they often do so in response to interest groups.

The Dance of Legislation

Bills become laws by a process that is simple in its outline. A bill may be introduced in either house. It is then assigned to a specialized committee, which may refer it to a subcommittee for closer study and modification. When the subcommittee has completed its work, it may send the proposal back to the full committee, which may then approve it and report it out to the chamber for debate, amendment, and a vote on passage. Actual floor procedures in the two houses differ substantially. In the House, the Rules Committee specifies the length and form of debate. In contrast, the Senate works within a tradition of unlimited debate and unanimous consent petitions. If a bill passes the two houses in different versions, the differences must be reconciled in a conference committee, and the bill must then be passed in its new form by each house. Once the bill has passed Congress, it is sent to the president for his signature, veto, or pocket veto. Though the process is simple to outline, the political reality is that thousands of bills may be introduced in a session of Congress, but only a few hundred ultimately become laws. Most bills die at the committee level.

Committees: The Workhorses of Congress

The real work of lawmaking happens in the legislative committees. The U.S. system of specialized standing committees allows members of Congress to build up expertise in issue areas as they build up seniority in Congress. Standing committees are broken down into subcommittees that allow members to acquire even more specialized expertise. Subcommittee members are often the dominant forces shaping legislation. In addition to their work on standing committees, members of Congress serve on joint committees made up of legislators from both houses; select committees established to deal with special issues; and conference committees, which work out differences between versions of legislation passed by the two houses. Leadership on committees is linked to seniority

In addition to its responsibility for passing new laws, Congress must also keep watch over the administration of existing laws. Through this oversight function, Congress is able to monitor existing policies and programs to see if agencies are carrying them out as Congress intended. Oversight occurs in various ways, including hearings, formal reports, and informal contacts between congressional and agency personnel. Since the 1970s, Congress has increased its oversight over the executive branch.

Reliance on a committee system decentralizes power and makes U.S. democracy more pluralistic; yet, there is a majoritarian aspect as well because most committees approximate the general profile of the parties' congressional membership, and legislation must still receive a majority vote in each house before becoming law.

Leaders and Followers in Congress

Each house has leaders who work to maximize their party's influence and keep their chamber functioning smoothly and efficiently. Party leadership in the House is exercised by the Speaker of the House and the minority leader. In the Senate, power is vested in the majority and minority leaders. These four leaders are selected by vote of their own party members in the chamber. Much of their work consists of persuasion and coalition building.

Each house has its own formal rules of procedure specifying how debates are conducted in that chamber. Debate in the House is limited, but the Senate has a longstanding tradition of unlimited debate, which creates the opportunity for a filibuster. In the classic filibuster, a senator attempted to talk a bill to death. In the modern filibuster, the Senate usually agrees to set aside an issue *as if* a Senator were conducting a classic filibuster. However, in the modern version, no one is actually forced to stand and talk about the bill. Business continues on other issues. In addition, each house also has unwritten, informal norms of behavior that help reduce conflict among people who often hold strongly opposing points of view but who must work together. Though some norms, such as the apprenticeship norm, have been weakened, successful members of Congress become adept at compromising to assemble coalitions of support for measures that interest them.

The Legislative Environment

Legislators look to four sources for their cues on how to vote on issues. First, rank-and-file party members usually try to support their party when they can, and partisanship has increased in recent years as each of the major parties has become more homogeneous. Second, the president is often actively engaged in trying to persuade legislators to vote his way. The views of the constituents back home are a third factor in how legislators vote. Finally, interest groups provide legislators with information on issues and their impact on the home district. These four influences push Congress in both the majoritarian and the pluralist directions.

The Dilemma of Representation

A central question for representative government is whether representatives should act as trustees who vote according to their consciences or as delegates who vote as their constituents wish them to vote. In the U.S. Congress, members feel a responsibility to both roles. A need to consider the larger national interest pushes them to act as trustees, while the need to face their constituents at the next election leads them to act more like delegates. By and large, members of Congress do not consistently adopt one role or the other.

Pluralism, Majoritarianism, and Democracy

The American Congress is quite different from a European parliament, where power is highly concentrated in the majority party in the legislative branch. Decentralization and the lack of a strong party system make Congress an institution better suited to pluralist democracy. Although aspects of the Contract with America represented a step toward majoritarian democracy, the House and Senate are still more pluralist than majoritarian.

KEY TERMS

reapportionment

impeachment

incumbent

gerrymandering

casework

descriptive representation

racial gerrymandering

veto

pocket veto

standing committee

joint committee

select committee

conference committee

seniority

oversight

Speaker of the House

majority leader

filibuster

cloture

constituents

trustee

delegate

parliamentary system

RESEARCH AND RESOURCES

In addition to the selected readings grouped at the end of the textbook, a useful starting point for research on how Congress operates is Walter J. Oleszek's *Congressional Procedures and the Policy Process*, 6th ed. (Washington, D.C.: Congressional Quarterly Press, 2004). This work includes a balanced but accessible treasure-trove of information on the powers and procedures of Congress, along with excellent analysis of how the institutional leadership's use of those procedures has evolved in recent years.

Two other *Congressional Quarterly* publications, *Directory of Congressional Voting Scores and Interest Group Ratings,* 4th ed., (Washington, D.C.: CQ Press, 2004) and *CQ's Guide to Current American Government* (published twice a year), are also helpful to those studying Congress. The former provides data on how members vote and how interest groups evaluate those votes. The latter volume provides a very helpful overview of key developments and debates within the policy world.

Suppose you need to find the actual text of a Senate floor debate or a House committee hearing. You'll want to turn to government documents. Floor debates are covered in the *Congressional Record*, published daily while Congress is in session and available on-line. To access it, try "Thomas," the congressional website site maintained by the Library of Congress, <http://thomas.loc.gov>. The *Congressional Record* may be searched on the Thomas site from 1989 to the present. The Government Printing Office allows you to search several types of legislative documents online as well, including bills, laws, and the daily *Congressional Record* from 1994 at <http://www.gpoaccess.gov/legislative.html>. Naturally, you will not want to skip <http://www.house.gov> or <http://www.senate.gov>.

A very useful non-governmental site for coverage of Congress is sponsored by *Rollcall*, the newspaper of Capitol Hill. It is available electronically on the Web by subscription at <http://www.rollcall.com>. Another excellent non-governmental resource is at <http://www.congress.org>. This site is sponsored by a Washington firm called Capital Advantage.

USING YOUR KNOWLEDGE

1.   Using Congressional Quarterly's *CQ Weekly* or the Internet resources suggested above, trace the legislation history of a bill passed by Congress in the last two years. When was the bill introduced? What were its major provisions? What committees examined it? Were there any major changes made by committees? What were they? Were there major amendments voted on during the floor debate?

2.   For a more extensive version of the above project, look up the House and Senate committee hearings on the bill. Who testified on behalf of the legislation? Who opposed it? What were the major arguments advanced by proponents and their opposition? Next, find the floor debates on the bill in the *Congressional Record.* Who supported the bill? Who opposed it? Why?

3.   Watch a House debate and a Senate debate on C-SPAN. What differences do you notice between the two? Next, watch a committee hearing. Describe the differences between committee hearings and floor debates.

4.   Watch the classic film *Mr. Smith Goes to Washington*, in which the protagonist resorts to a classic filibuster to address a grave injustice. Then use an Internet search engine such as Google.com or Altavista.com to locate articles with all three of these terms: "filibuster," "Mansfield," and "two-

track." Describe how and why the filibuster changed. What advantages has the modern filibuster brought to the Senate, and what has been lost?

GETTING INVOLVED

If you would like to have a chance to learn more about the life of a representative or senator, you might begin by contacting your own congressional representatives. They may welcome part-time volunteer help in their offices in the home district, or they may have internships available in their Washington offices. You can find contact information at <http://www.house.gov> or <http://www.senate.gov>.

SAMPLE EXAM QUESTIONS

Multiple-Choice Questions

1. Both the House and Senate
   a. may try impeachments.
   b. vote on declarations of war.
   c. may originate revenue bills.
   d. ratify treaties.
2. Elected officials are drawn disproportionately from the ranks of
   a. college-educated white males.
   b. professional women.
   c. Hispanics.
   d. blue-collar white males.
3. When a president vetoes a bill, it
   a. cannot be reconsidered in that session of Congress.
   b. becomes law if it can be passed again by at least three-fourths of the membership of each house.
   c. becomes law if it can be passed again by at least two-thirds of those voting in each house.
   d. becomes law if it can be passed again by a simple majority in each house.
4. The idea that the best representatives of a particular group, gender, or race are people who belong to it is called
   a. descriptive representation.
   b. racial gerrymandering.
   c. the trusteeship theory of representation.
   d. the delegate theory of representation.
5. The legislative agenda is shaped by
   a. the president.
   b. party leaders and committee chairs.
   c. new issues and events.
   d. All of the above.
6. A permanent committee specializing in a particular area of legislative policy is called a
   a. standing committee.
   b. steering committee.
   c. select committee.
   d. conference committee.

7.   The temporary committee to investigate a problem is probably a

   a.   standing committee.
   b.   select committee.
   c.   joint committee.
   d.   conference committee.

8.   On congressional committees, the chair is usually occupied by

   a.   the senior minority member.
   b.   the senior majority member.
   c.   a member selected by all committee members in an open, democratic process.
   d.   a member from the most populous state.

9.   Which of the following features of the committee system tends to make it more of a pluralist than a majoritarian device?

   a.   Decentralization
   b.   Specialization
   c.   Congressional attention to the interests of the district
   d.   All of the above.

10.   In the Senate, the greatest power resides in the office of

   a.   majority leader.
   b.   minority leader.
   c.   vice president.
   d.   president pro tempore.

11.   Which of the following might be used in a debate in the House of Representatives but not in the Senate?

   a.   A rule on germaneness
   b.   A unanimous consent agreement
   c.   A filibuster
   d.   A cloture vote

12.   The Senate's tradition of unlimited debate promotes

   a.   equality.
   b.   order.
   c.   pluralism.
   d.   majoritarianism.

13.   Redrawing the boundaries of an electoral district in an irregular shape to favor a particular party or candidate is called

   a.   logrolling.
   b.   gerrymandering.
   c.   pairing.
   d.   filibustering.

14.   Congressman A is a forty-five-year-old white devout Christian, strongly opposed to any form of legalized abortion. He polls his mostly white, middle-class constituency and discovers that the majority in his district consistently opposes legislation making abortions more difficult to obtain. He decides to follow his conscience and votes for legislation limiting the availability of abortion under Medicaid. Which of the following best accounts for his choice?

   a.   The theory of majoritarianism
   b.   The idea of descriptive representation
   c.   The view of representatives as delegates
   d.   The view of representatives as trustees

15. The common name for the process of reviewing agency operations to determine whether an agency is carrying out policies as Congress intended is called
    a. oversight.
    b. legislative review.
    c. judicial review.
    d. germaneness.

16. The number of representatives to which states are entitled in the House of Representatives
    a. was fixed permanently when each state joined the Union.
    b. changes to reflect voter turnout in each election.
    c. is revised every five years based on the quinquennial census.
    d. is revised every ten years based on the decennial census.

17. Which of the following actions is *not* specifically authorized in the Constitution?
    a. The president using the line-item veto to reject part of a bill
    b. The president signing a bill into law
    c. The president vetoing a bill
    d. The president pocket vetoing a bill by failing to sign it at the end of a legislative session

18. Impeachment is a power
    a. to charge an official with treason, bribery, or other high crimes or misdemeanors.
    b. to try an official charged with treason, bribery, or other high crimes or misdemeanors.
    c. to remove from office an official convicted of treason, bribery, or other high crimes or misdemeanors.
    d. that has not been used in this century.

19. Representatives who seek re-election rarely lose. This phenomenon is known as
    a. racial gerrymandering.
    b. redistricting.
    c. the incumbency effect.
    d. the seniority system.

20. In comparison with members of the House, senators seeking re-election find that
    a. incumbency is usually less of an advantage.
    b. incumbency is usually more of an advantage.
    c. gerrymandering is more important.
    d. redistricting is more often a disadvantage.

Essay Questions

1. What advantages does incumbency give a member of the House of Representatives? Is incumbency as great an advantage to senators? Why or why not?

2. Some people have argued that to be truly representative, a legislature should mirror the characteristics of the people it is supposed to represent. Is the U.S. Congress representative in this sense? Give specific examples concerning the extent to which Congress mirrors the general population with respect to race, gender, education, and occupational status.

3. Does the congressional committee system, as it operates, better fit the pluralist or majoritarian model of democracy?

4. Discuss the major influences that help legislators decide how to vote on particular issues.

5. Distinguish between the trustee and the delegate roles of representatives. Which role, if either, tends to be more characteristic of U.S. legislators?

ANSWERS TO MULTIPLE-CHOICE QUESTIONS

1. b
2. a
3. c
4. a
5. d
6. a
7. b
8. b
9. d
10. a
11. a
12. c
13. b
14. d
15. a
16. d
17. a
18. a
19. c
20. a

CHAPTER 9

The Presidency

LEARNING OBJECTIVES

After reading this chapter you should be able to

- Define the key terms identified in the chapter margins.

- List the powers and duties of the president, as set forth in the Constitution.

- Describe other sources that presidents have used to expand the authority of the office.

- Explain why modern presidents are more likely to rely on the White House staff than on the cabinet for advice on policymaking.

- Discuss the factors enabling presidents to exercise political leadership.

- Point out the assets and liabilities a president brings with him as he tries to translate his political vision into public policy.

- Explain what referring to the president as "chief lobbyist" means.

- Discuss the factors requiring U.S. presidents to exercise leadership in world affairs.

- Describe the special skills presidents need for crisis management.

THE PRESIDENCY AND THE CHALLENGE OF DEMOCRACY

Despite the obstacles created by checks and balances and the separation of powers, the president enjoys a substantial set of powers defined in the Constitution. Perhaps the most dramatic of these is his role as commander-in-chief. As the opening vignette about the war in Iraq pointed out, the use of these powers can transform a presidency. After the September 11 attacks on the United States, President George W. Bush's public approval ratings skyrocketed. As President Bush discovered when he pushed the "war on terror" into Iraq to topple Saddam Hussein, public opinion can be a fickle friend. With the declaration that major combat operations were over, the military mission in Iraq was transformed into an effort to reestablish stability and security in the face of a mounting insurgency. Approval of Bush's actions plummeted.

The president and vice president are the only nationally elected political officials in the United States. As a result, there is strong moral pressure on the president to be "the president of all the people." The president is potentially the focal point of majoritarian politics in the U.S. system. He is in a unique position to see that the national interest is not always the sum of all our single or special interests. Following opinion polls may make him aware of the need to appeal to the majority. Yet, the realities of U.S. presidential politics are more pluralistic than majoritarian. Although classical majoritarian theory might put a premium on being responsible to "the people," the reality of presidential politics is that people to whom presidents respond are organized in groups.

CHAPTER OVERVIEW

The task of designing the office of chief executive presented the founders with a dilemma. They had just rebelled against a king and were naturally reluctant to concentrate too much power in the hands of one individual. Yet, their experience under the Articles of Confederation convinced them that strong national leadership was needed. So they established the office of president—a position filled by one person chosen independently of Congress by indirect election through the electoral college. To limit presidential power, they relied on two factors: the mechanism of checks and balances and their expectation that the anticipated first incumbent, George Washington, would set good precedents.

The Constitutional Basis of Presidential Power

According to the Constitution, the president is the administrative head of the nation and the commander-in-chief of the armed forces. He has the power to convene Congress and to grant pardons. Subject to various congressional limitations, he may veto legislation passed by Congress; appoint ambassadors, judges, cabinet members, and other key officials; and make treaties.

The Expansion of Presidential Power

Presidents have become more aggressive in their use of the formal powers granted in the Constitution. The list of the president's constitutional powers does not tell the whole story, however. Presidential power has increased tremendously since the Constitution was adopted. The expansion of presidential power resulted from claims that the president has certain inherent powers implied by the Constitution, such as the power to remove cabinet officers. In addition, Congress has also delegated power to the executive branch, allowing the president more freedom to implement policies.

The Executive Branch Establishment

The executive branch establishment gives a president substantial resources to translate an electoral mandate into public policy. He may call on the executive office of the president, the cabinet, or the vice president, or he may rely on his own staff, including his national security adviser, Council of Economic Advisers, and the Office of Management and Budget. The methods presidents use to organize their staffs differ from administration to administration and generally reflect the individual chief executive's own working style. Modern presidents usually rely much more heavily on the White House staff than on the cabinet (the heads of the executive departments and other officials) to make policy. In theory, the cabinet also acts as a presidential advisory group, but the importance of the cabinet has declined as the importance of the White House staff has grown. Traditionally, presidents have rarely looked to their vice presidents for assistance on substantive policy matters. This changed beginning with the Carter administration. Presidents Clinton and Bush have both leaned heavily upon their vice presidents for advice and support.

Presidential Leadership

A president's leadership is a function of his character, skills, and political environment. Though character is often hard to judge, the public clearly thinks that it matters. Much of the discussion surrounding the impeachment of President Clinton focused on character issues.

The president's ability to persuade is one of the most important factors determining how much power he has. His persuasiveness is often related to his personality but may also result from his professional reputation and public prestige. These attributes, in turn, spring from factors such as past successes (at the polls or with Congress) and presidential popularity. Presidential popularity may be affected by many factors, including economic conditions, wars, and unanticipated events. Presidents usually are at the peak of their popularity during the "honeymoon period" of their first year in office, and they monitor their popularity closely as a kind of "report card." Good communication can serve to rally the public to the president's side when he "goes public," but the ability to form congressional and interest group coalitions should not be overlooked either.

Divided government, with the presidency and Congress controlled by different parties, has made it more difficult in recent years for presidents to translate perceived mandates into policy, although polls suggest that the public prefers to have control of government divided between Democrats and Republicans, and scholars are divided in their assessment of the productivity of divided government.

The President as National Leader

Presidents have differed considerably in their views of what government should do. Some, like Lyndon Johnson, emphasized the value of equality, while others, including Ronald Reagan, stressed freedom. The agendas they set grow out of their general political ideologies, tempered by the realities of political life in Washington. In the modern era, presidents have assumed significant leadership in the legislative process. Departments and agencies clear their budgets and proposed legislation through the president. Presidents also act as "chief lobbyists," trying to win support in Congress for their proposals. In this role, presidents may rely on their own personal contact with legislators, on contacts by their legislative liaison staffs, or on the aid of interest groups. Presidents may also use the threat of a veto as leverage to prevent Congress from passing measures of which they disapprove.

In addition to serving as national leader, a president is also the leader of his party. However, close party ties do not always characterize U.S. presidents.

The President as World Leader

By virtue of the position of the United States in the world, the president is not only a national leader, but he is also a world leader. In foreign relations, presidents have four general objectives: (1) protecting the national security of the United States, (2) fostering a peaceful international environment, (3) protecting U.S. economic interests, and (4) promoting democracy around the globe. As a world leader, he must rely on his powers of persuasion; during periods of crisis he needs good judgment and coolness under pressure. As globalization and interdependence have increased in the aftermath of the Cold War, presidents find themselves paying more attention to the connection between foreign policy and domestic politics. This is especially true where economic relations are concerned.

KEY TERMS

veto

inherent powers

executive orders

delegation of powers

Executive Office of the President

cabinet

divided government

gridlock

mandate

legislative liaison staff

RESEARCH AND RESOURCES

For up-to-date information on the president's policies and actions, the best official source is the *Weekly Compilation of Presidential Documents* (Washington, D.C.: U.S. Government Printing Office), which is published every Monday by the Office of the Federal Register. Issues of this publication since 1993 are available on the Web at <http://www.access.gpo.gov/nara/nara003.html>.

In addition to this resource, the Federal Register also issues an annual bound volume entitled *Public Papers of the Presidents of the United States* (Washington, D.C.: U.S. Government Printing Office). These volumes are useful for researching the presidency from Truman's administration to the present. The contents of the Federal Register since 1994 are available on-line at <http://www.gpoaccess.gov/fr/index.html>.

If you wish to study earlier occupants of the White House, you should turn to *A Compilation of the Messages and Papers of the Presidents, 1789–1927* (New York: Bureau of National Literature, 1928). This is a twenty-volume set containing official utterances of presidents from Washington to Coolidge. These volumes include presidential proclamations, addresses, annual messages, veto messages, and other communications to Congress, as well as articles about the issues that faced each president.

For the interim period not covered by either of the two works above, you will find the following two privately published works useful:

Hoover, Herbert C. *The State Papers and Other Public Writings of Herbert Hoover*. Garden City, NY: Doubleday, Doran & Co., 1934.

Roosevelt, Franklin. *The Public Papers and Addresses of Franklin D. Roosevelt*. New York: Random House, 1938–1950.

For current on-line information, the White House maintains its own Web site at <http://www.whitehouse.gov>. You can read about the president and vice president, search presidential documents, check out current press releases, listen to speeches, and even tour the White House from your desktop. If you are interested in historical information on individual presidents, including sound and video clips, another resource to check out is "Grolier Online's The American Presidency" at <http://ap.grolier.com/>.

USING YOUR KNOWLEDGE

1.   Using the resources suggested above, try to learn the president's position on the bill you researched in Chapter 8. Were there speeches or press conferences where he indicated his views on the bill? Was there a public ceremony where he delivered remarks as he signed the bill into law? Was there a veto message?

2.   Use Gallup Poll data to construct a line graph showing the percentage of respondents who approved of the way President George Bush handled his job from 1989-1993. Do you observe any trends in your graph? How do the trends in your graph compare with the usual trend in presidential popularity sketched out in the text? Try the same exercise for Presidents Bill Clinton and George W. Bush during their first terms and compare the results.

3.   Have you ever wanted to tell the president what you think? Pick up your phone and dial 1-202-456-1111, the White House comment line. If you want to talk to someone on the staff, you'll need to call the White House switchboard at 202-456-1414. To send electronic mail to the president, write to president@whitehouse.gov. Of course, you are extremely unlikely to find the occupant of the Oval Office answering his own phone or responding to his own e-mail, but you can register your opinion on issues that are of significance to you. The White House uses both to track public opinion.

GETTING INVOLVED

One of the most prestigious and competitive opportunities for students in Washington, D.C., is the White House internship program. It offers interns the opportunity to work in one of twenty-six White

House offices, handling a range of chores from advance planning to staffing the visitors' office. Internships are available for spring, summer, or fall sessions. For deadlines and further information, see <http://www.whitehouse.gov/government/wh-intern.html>.

SAMPLE EXAM QUESTIONS

Multiple-Choice Questions

1. A president's power to persuade is

    a. specified in the Constitution.
    b. less important than his constitutional powers.
    c. often related to his popularity.
    d. not useful in distinguishing between mediocre and above-average presidents.

2. Congressional delegation of power

    a. gives Congress more power to specify the details of policy.
    b. lets the executive have more latitude to implement policies.
    c. may not be rescinded without a two-thirds vote of both houses of Congress.
    d. has little impact on the balance of power between the executive and the legislature.

3. Which of the following is *not* included among the fundamental objectives of presidential foreign policy in the twenty-first century?

    a. Supporting world court supervision of troops in multilateral peacekeeping exercises
    b. Protecting the national security of the United States
    c. Promoting democracy around the globe
    d. Fostering a peaceful international environment

4. The Constitution empowers the president to act in all of the following ways *except* as

    a. administrative head of the union.
    b. chief of his political party.
    c. commander-in-chief of the military.
    d. treaty maker.

5. When government is unable to act on policy issues, the situation is described as

    a. a congressional mandate.
    b. a presidential mandate.
    c. gridlock.
    d. downsizing.

6. Article II of the Constitution explicitly gives the president the power to

    a. appoint and remove Supreme Court Justices.
    b. veto legislation on a line-by-line basis.
    c. convene Congress.
    d. All of the above.

7. The Constitution gives the power to declare war to

    a. the president.
    b. the president, with the advice and consent of the Senate.
    c. Congress.
    d. the president, on the advice of the National Security Council.

8.   When a president claims that the voters have given him a special endorsement of his policies in an election, he is claiming

   a.   inherent powers.
   b.   a mandate.
   c.   a congressional delegation of power.
   d.   veto power.

9.   Which of the following has *not* been a major factor in increasing presidential power?

   a.   Constitutional amendments expanding presidential power
   b.   The theory of inherent presidential power
   c.   Crises such as war or depression
   d.   Congressional delegations of power

10.   In recent times, most presidents have relied most heavily for advice on which of the following?

   a.   The First Lady
   b.   The White House staff
   c.   The cabinet
   d.   The Senate

11.   The White House staff

   a.   is strictly limited in size.
   b.   must be confirmed by the Senate.
   c.   consists of people loyal to the president and hence rarely suffers from turf wars.
   d.   has no set advisory structure and reflects the president's own style of organization.

12.   In attempting to translate his political vision into new legislation, a president may

   a.   count on a "honeymoon" effect through his first term.
   b.   use the line-item veto to reject parts of bills that don't fit in with his philosophy.
   c.   use liaison staff and interest groups to pressure Congress.
   d.   not involve himself in the legislative process once his bills are introduced.

13.   According to Richard Neustadt, the key presidential power is the

   a.   veto power.
   b.   power of the purse.
   c.   power to persuade.
   d.   appointment power.

14.   During a president's first year in office, his program may stand a better chance of passage due to the

   a.   nature of divided government.
   b.   fact that one house of Congress will be controlled by the president's party.
   c.   fact that both houses of Congress will be controlled by the president's party.
   d.   "honeymoon" effect.

15.   The situation in which one party controls Congress while the other party controls the White House is known as

   a.   the separation of powers.
   b.   checks and balances.
   c.   pluralism.
   d.   divided government.

16. As originally ratified, the Constitution included which of the following among its requirements for presidential candidates?

    a.   A natural born citizen who has lived in the United States for at least fourteen years
    b.   A male at least thirty-five years of age
    c.   A white male at least thirty-five years of age
    d.   A property owner

17. According to the text, one defense of presidential concern with public opinion is that it

    a.   may lead to government that is more responsive to the majority.
    b.   may lead to government that is more responsive to special interests.
    c.   results in more principled leadership.
    d.   promotes equality.

18. The contemporary role of the president in the legislative process is best described as one in which

    a.   the president proposes and Congress disposes.
    b.   under the separation of powers, the president distances himself from the process.
    c.   the president may serve as chief lobbyist, active in all stages of legislation.
    d.   the president is active only if his party controls Congress.

19. The day-to-day communications link between the president and Congress is the

    a.   legislative liaison staff.
    b.   vice president.
    c.   cabinet.
    d.   Office of Management and Budget.

20. Modern presidents are less likely to rely on their cabinets to make policy because

    a.   the cabinet is too large and unwieldy to be a good policymaking body.
    b.   cabinet members have limited areas of expertise. The secretary of agriculture may know very little about housing policy, for example.
    c.   presidents have large White House staffs to take on this advisory role.
    d.   All of the above.

Essay Questions

1.   Does divided government mean gridlock? Draw on research discussed in the chapter in formulating your answer.

2.   What is the popular image of the presidency? How has this image created an impossible task for occupants of the Oval Office?

3.   Explain the devices presidents have used to extend their power in areas where they were not given power by the Constitution.

4.   Discuss the factors that help make presidents persuasive.

5.   Discuss the president's constitutional powers in foreign policy and the roles he plays by virtue of the U.S. superpower status on the global stage.

ANSWERS TO MULTIPLE-CHOICE QUESTIONS

1. c
2. b
3. a
4. b
5. c
6. c
7. c
8. b
9. a
10. b
11. d
12. c
13. c
14. d
15. d
16. a
17. a
18. c
19. a
20. d

CHAPTER 10

The Bureaucracy

LEARNING OBJECTIVES

After reading this chapter you should be able to

- Define the key terms identified in the chapter margins.

- List key factors that have contributed to the growth of the U.S. bureaucracy.

- Explain the difficulties that surround efforts to reduce the size of the bureaucracy.

- Outline the basic types of organizations that make up the bureaucracy.

- Explain why presidents often feel that they have inadequate control of the bureaucracy.

- Describe the formal and informal processes of bureaucratic policymaking.

- Explain the "rational comprehensive" model of decision making and compare it with real-world decision making.

- Give the main reasons why policies fail at the implementation stage.

- Discuss the difference between the various strategies to reform the bureaucracy.

THE BUREAUCRACY AND THE CHALLENGE OF DEMOCRACY

The cumulative failures of executive branch agencies to prevent the September 11 attack on the United States illustrates the dilemma created by Americans' rejecting big government but wanting the protection big government provides. Every day, through the bureaucracy, the government is involved in hundreds of situations that involve conflicts among the values of freedom, order, and equality. Departments, bureaus, and agencies are required to make rules, to adjudicate, and to exercise administrative discretion to fill in the details left out of legislation passed by Congress. Their mandates are often broad and their budgets constrained. Do government agencies have the resources necessary to achieve legislative goals? Does the bureaucracy try to do too much? Is it out of control and out of touch?

From a majoritarian standpoint, the answers to these questions is mixed. In recent years, the public has shown a preference for a smaller bureaucracy, but the demands on bureaucracy have expanded. Once again we see the impact of pluralism on the U.S. system. The various bureaus, agencies, and departments exist to do what some part of the population (call it a faction or an interest group) wants government to do. Often, the bureaucracy balances competing interests, thus doing a job that political scientists think is essential if pluralism is to be democratic.

Efforts to reform the bureaucracy may run into trouble because of pluralist politics. Interest groups that have built up contacts with existing agencies will fight reorganization. Deregulation offers another method of reducing the bureaucracy, but it raises anew the fundamental question of values: it may provide greater freedom, but it may also result in inadequate protection, thus undermining order.

CHAPTER OVERVIEW

Organization Matters

The large, complex mass of organizations that administer the nation's laws and implement government policy is known as the bureaucracy. Although there is no one best way to structure all bureaucracies, it is clear that a bureaucracy's organization directly affects its ability to perform effectively.

Development of the Bureaucratic State

Government at all levels grew enormously in the twentieth century. This growth resulted from several factors:

- Increased complexity, which changed society's attitudes about government's role in the marketplace

- Changed attitudes about government's social welfare responsibilities

- Ambitious officials who wish to expand their organizations to serve their clients more fully

On the whole, the public has little confidence in the government, but cuts in the government's size are difficult because each part of the bureaucracy does a job some part of society wants done. Interest groups with a stake in an agency or department will often organize to resist cuts.

Bureaus and Bureaucrats

The bureaucracy is not a unified entity but a collection of dozens of government organizations, including the following:

- Fifteen departments—cabinet-level organizations that cover broad areas of government responsibility and contain within them numerous subsidiary offices and bureaus. The largest of these is the Department of Defense. The most recently created is the Department of Homeland Security.

- Independent agencies and regulatory commissions—not part of any cabinet department and controlled to varying degrees by the president

- Government corporations—organizations that provide services, such as mail delivery and passenger rail, that could be provided by the private sector but have been made public because Congress decided it better serves the public interest

Most of the approximately 2.7 million workers in the federal bureaucracy are part of the civil service, a system established to fill government jobs on the basis of merit rather than political patronage. The overall composition of the federal bureaucracy generally mirrors the population, although higher-level policymaking positions tend to be dominated by white males.

Among the members of the bureaucracy, 99 percent are protected from party politics by civil service status; the remaining 1 percent of positions are filled by people appointed by the president. Although presidential appointees fill the top policymaking jobs, the bulk of civil service employees are independent of the chief executive. Therefore, presidents often feel that they are unable to exert control over the bureaucracy and use it to achieve their purposes. Presidents' efforts to control the bureaucracy often fall short partly because bureaucracies respond to other constituencies besides the president.

Administrative Policymaking: The Formal Processes

Congress gives the cabinet-level departments and agencies it creates administrative discretion—that is, authority to make policy within certain guidelines. Sometimes, the guidelines are vague. The wide latitude Congress gives the bureaucracy sometimes leads to charges that the government is out of control. But Congress does have the power to review the legislation that establishes bureaucratic organizations. It also controls the purse strings. Informal contacts between members of Congress and agency personnel also help Congress communicate its intentions to the bureaucracy.

Administrative discretion is exercised through rule making—the quasi-legislative process of formulating and issuing regulations. Regulations are created to implement and enforce the laws passed by the Congress and have the force of law. They are created in accordance with a formal procedure that allows affected parties to register their views. Regulations serve to balance the needs of society.

Administrative Policymaking: Informal Politics

Real-world decision making in government does not really resemble the textbook "rational-comprehensive" model, in which administrators rank their objectives and carefully weigh the costs and benefits of all possible solutions to a problem. In practice, policymakers find that their values often conflict—that their time, information, and options are limited, and the decisions that are best in theory may in reality be politically impractical. Policymaking becomes a matter of "muddling through" and tends to be incremental, with policies changing only very gradually over time.

Bureaucracies develop written rules and regulations to promote efficiency and fairness. In addition, certain unwritten rules and norms evolve, influencing the way people act on the job. Employees in a bureaucracy—the bureaucrats—wish to advance their careers, and as a result they may avoid rocking the boat—that is, engaging in behavior that might violate written or unwritten canons.

Problems in Implementing Policy

Policies do not always accomplish what they are designed to accomplish. To find out why, it is necessary to look beyond the process of policymaking, to policy implementation. Policies may fail because the directives concerning them or their implementation may be vague or because lower-level officials have too much discretion. Programs may fail because of the complexity of government: the necessary coordination among federal agencies or among federal, state, and local agencies may be impossible to achieve. Policies may also fail because policymakers overestimate the capacity of an agency to carry them out.

Reforming the Bureaucracy: More Control or Less?

Because organization makes a difference in a bureaucracy's ability to achieve its goals, people in government often tinker with organizational designs to make bureaucracy more effective. But what method of "reinventing" or streamlining the government is best? Would the bureaucracy work better if controls over it were tighter or looser? Earlier efforts to reform the bureaucracy emphasized deregulation. Deregulation is an effort to lessen government intervention in the workings of business and markets. Freedom from regulation enhances firms' and individuals' ability to compete in the marketplace, but without regulation there is little to ensure that they will act responsibly. In order to encourage government agencies to act more efficiently, some conservative critics advocate a competitive approach. This view suggests that if government cannot carry out a function efficiently, it should outsource the task to private companies. Other reformers stress government responsiveness and promote total quality management (TQM), a model borrowed from business. Just as businesses aim at customer satisfaction under this model, government works to satisfy its citizens. A fourth approach to bureaucratic reform is to promote better performance of governmental agencies through setting performance goals and holding agencies accountable.

KEY TERMS

bureaucracy

bureaucrat

department

independent agency

regulatory commission

government corporation

civil service

administrative discretion

rule making

regulations

incrementalism

norms

implementation

regulation

deregulation

competition and outsourcing

total quality management (TQM)

Government Performance and Results Act

RESEARCH AND RESOURCES

The U.S. government bureaucracy is large and complex, but there are some good reference tools to help you make sense of it. The *United States Government Manual*, published annually and billed as the official handbook of the federal government, contains detailed information on all three branches of government as well as extensive material on departments and agencies. Typically, a description of an agency provides a list of its principal officials, a summary of its purposes and role in the government, an outline of its legislative or executive functions, and a description of its activities. In the back, the manual offers organizational charts of the agencies it describes. It is now available on the Internet in searchable form at <http://www.gpoaccess.gov/gmanual/index.html>.

To find specific federal regulations on-line, you might search the *Code of Federal Regulations* at <http://www.gpoaccess.gov/cfr/index.html>. For Web links to specific departments, agencies, and offices in the executive branch, try <http://www.lcweb.loc.gov/global/executive/fed.html>.

Congressional Quarterly's *Federal Regulatory Directory,* 12th ed. (Washington, D.C.: Congressional Quarterly Press, 2006) contains much of the same information found in the *United States Government Manual*, although the *Federal Regulatory Directory* is not updated as frequently. It does have some other useful features, however. It opens with an introductory essay on the regulatory process, exploring the history of regulation and current trends and issues. It contains detailed profiles on major regulatory agencies, including analyses of their past histories, current issues, and future prospects. Brief biographical sketches of major administrators within each agency are also included.

USING YOUR KNOWLEDGE

1. Using the *Federal Regulatory Directory* and the *United States Government Manual*, prepare a profile of a government agency. Outline its functions, present status, and future prospects. How large is its budget? How many people does it employ? Have these figures increased or decreased? Have its responsibilities grown or decreased recently?

2. Examine the organizational charts at the back of the *United States Government Manual*. As you look at various charts, make notes on areas of responsibility of the different departments that seem to overlap. (For example, the Departments of Housing and Urban Development, Health and Human Services, and the Interior all contain offices dealing with aspects of Indian affairs.) Try to come up with other examples. What are the pluses and minuses of a system that allows this kind of overlap? What difficulties might you expect to encounter if you were to attempt reorganization? Which model of democracy fits well with this type of organization?

GETTING INVOLVED

As the chapter noted, the national government employs people all over the country in almost every field imaginable. If you are interested in government, you may want to consider a career working in one of the many departments, bureaus, or agencies of the federal system. As we noted in the text, all federal government employees (except for a very few political employees at the highest levels) are part of the civil service merit system. What should you do if you are interested in joining their ranks?

In the past, the Office of Personnel Management played the biggest role in the hiring process, but now the process is more decentralized. This means that in addition to visiting the Federal Job Information Center in your area and filling out Standard Form 171 (SF 171), the basic résumé form required to apply for most federal jobs, you'll also want to contact particular agencies where you think your talents and interests could be put to use.

Many useful resources can help you learn more about the federal job-seeking process. Here is a brief bibliography:

Damp, Dennis V. *The Book of U.S. Government Jobs: Where They Are, What's Available & How to Get One*, 9th rev. ed. (Moon Township, Penn.: Brookhaven Press, 2005).

Troutman, Kathryn. *The Student's Federal Career Guide: Ten Steps to Find and Win Top Government Jobs and Internships* (Baltimore: The Resumè Place, 2004).

Even if you do not plan to seek employment with the federal government, remember that many executive branch departments and agencies—from the Central Intelligence Agency to the Department of Housing and Urban Development—take interns. Information is available online at each organization's website. Use <http://www.lcweb.loc.gov/global/executive/fed.html> to get started.

SAMPLE EXAM QUESTIONS

Multiple-Choice Questions

1. The growth of the bureaucracy
   a. stopped during the Reagan years.
   b. is the result of the impact of majoritarian democracy.
   c. has resulted from the increased complexity of society as well as changed attitudes about business.
   d. All of the above.

2. A bureaucracy is generally
    a. large.
    b. hierarchically organized.
    c. filled with employees with specific job descriptions.
    d. All of the above.
3. The practice of filling government jobs with political allies or cronies is called
    a. total quality management.
    b. incrementalism.
    c. patronage.
    d. affirmative action.
4. The largest units of the executive branch, whose heads are members of the president's cabinet, are called
    a. departments.
    b. bureaus.
    c. regulatory commissions.
    d. independent agencies.
5. Regulatory commissions
    a. are totally immune to political pressure.
    b. may be indirectly influenced by presidents through their appointment power.
    c. may not be lobbied by interest groups.
    d. include Amtrak and the U.S. Postal Service.
6. The federal bureaucracy is made up primarily of a work force that
    a. is hired under a patronage system.
    b. works mainly in Washington, D.C.
    c. is hired without reference to political affiliations.
    d. overrepresents women and minorities in policymaking positions.
7. The civil service fills jobs based on
    a. merit selection criteria.
    b. ideological agreement with the administration.
    c. patronage.
    d. political party affiliation.
8. The latitude Congress gives agencies to make policy consistent with their organizational missions is called
    a. administrative discretion.
    b. patronage.
    c. analytical budgeting.
    d. implementation.
9. The formal administrative procedure that results in the issuance of regulations is called
    a. adjudication.
    b. rule making.
    c. reorganization.
    d. incrementalism.
10. Presidential appointees account for approximately what percentage of executive-branch employees?
    a. Less than 1 percent
    b. 8 to 10 percent
    c. 27.3 percent
    d. More than 50 percent

11. Federal regulations are often

    a.   made in a closed and secretive process.
    b.   the result of an agency's attempt to balance competing interests.
    c.   written in plain English to make them easily comprehensible.
    d.   less effective than laws.

12. The informal, unwritten rules of behavior that develop in bureaucracies are called

    a.   regulations.
    b.   norms.
    c.   esprit de corps.
    d.   administrative discretion.

13. Real-world administrative decisions are made in a process best described

    a.   by the "rational-comprehensive" model.
    b.   as incremental or "muddling through."
    c.   as immune from political pressure.
    d.   as rooted in cost-benefit analysis.

14. According to the text, policies sometimes fail at the implementation stage because

    a.   policy directives are unclear.
    b.   coordination among implementing agencies is weak.
    c.   policymakers have unrealistic expectations about an agency's capabilities.
    d.   All of the above.

15. All of the following are currently executive departments *except* the

    a.   Department of Veterans' Affairs.
    b.   Department of the Post Office.
    c.   Department of Justice.
    d.   Department of Transportation.

16. The main objective of the civil service merit system was to reduce

    a.   patronage.
    b.   competence.
    c.   decentralization.
    d.   pork barrel politics.

17. The rational-comprehensive model is criticized as being unrealistic because it overlooks the fact that

    a.   policymakers have difficulty defining goals and agreeing on their priorities.
    b.   the policies that are the best possible means to an end may not be politically palatable.
    c.   policymakers act with incomplete information under time pressure.
    d.   All of the above.

18. Presidents often claim that they do not have adequate control over the bureaucracy because

    a.   99 percent of agency employees are nonpolitical.
    b.   bureaucracy grows too quickly.
    c.   growth of the White House staff is strictly limited by law.
    d.   turnover rates within bureaucracies are too high.

19. An approach to managing the bureaucracy that treats agencies' clients like customers is

    a.   a planning-programming-budgeting system.
    b.   total quality management.
    c.   management by objective.
    d.   incrementalism.

20. The newest cabinet level department in the federal government is the
    a. Department of Housing and Urban Development.
    b. Department of Health and Human Services.
    c. Department of Homeland Security.
    d. Department of Environmental Preparedness.

Essay Questions

1. Why was the civil service system introduced? Why is the system often frustrating to presidents?

2. What key problems are associated with administrative discretion?

3. Outline the pros and cons of deregulation in theory and in recent practice.

4. Outline and explain the factors that have contributed to the growth of the bureaucracy.

5. Outline and explain the various strategies proposed to reform the bureaucracy. What are the political motivations driving the proponents of each strategy?

ANSWERS TO MULTIPLE-CHOICE QUESTIONS

1. c
2. d
3. c
4. a
5. b
6. c
7. a
8. a
9. b
10. a
11. b
12. b
13. b
14. d
15. b
16. a
17. d
18. a
19. b
20. c

CHAPTER 11

The Courts

LEARNING OBJECTIVES

After reading this chapter you should be able to

- Define the key terms identified in the chapter margins.

- Explain the concept of judicial review and how it was established in *Marbury* v. *Madison*.

- Sketch the basic organization of the federal court system.

- Explain the role of the federal district courts and federal appeals courts.

- Describe two ways in which judges exercise a policymaking role.

- Outline the routes by which cases come to the Supreme Court.

- Describe the formal procedures by which the Supreme Court reaches decisions.

- Explain ways in which justices, particularly the chief justice, influence court decisions.

- Describe the process of appointment to the federal judiciary.

- Evaluate the Supreme Court as an instrument of pluralist or majoritarian democracy.

THE COURTS AND THE CHALLENGE OF DEMOCRACY

In the U.S. system, the courts interpret the law. Courts are made up of judges, and judges bring their own value systems with them to the job. Each judge will give a different weight to freedom, order, and equality. Because federal judges hold lifetime appointments to insulate them from politics, a president's judicial appointees will continue to make decisions long after the president leaves office. They may do so without regard for the will of the majority. While a president may select judges on the basis of how well their values match his, the stakes are high, and he may find his nominees opposed by groups who oppose his values. The Supreme Court's role in deciding the 2000 presidential election offers a particularly pointed example of the stakes.

When judges interpret laws and precedents loosely in ways that are heavily influenced by their own values, they are said to be judicial activists. When they stick closely to the letter of the law and let their own preferences intrude as little as possible, they are said to exercise judicial restraint. Is judicial activism compatible with democracy? Sometimes, it has promoted democratic ends—as in the "one person, one vote" decisions, for example. But the judiciary itself is the least democratic branch of government. Its members are protected from popular control. They are appointed, not elected, and they serve life terms. Through judicial review, the Supreme Court may, and has, overruled acts of the popularly elected Congress. These attributes of the judiciary may seem undemocratic. However, as one commentator put it, in general the Supreme Court follows the election returns and doesn't go very far beyond the views of the public. But sometimes, as in the case of the school prayer decision, the Court may uphold a position opposed by a majority of the people. So the Court may act as a countermajoritarian force.

CHAPTER OVERVIEW

In U.S. democracy, the court system is involved in many decisions. Yet, the courts themselves are largely beyond democratic control. Judges are limited by statutes and precedents, but they still have substantial leeway in deciding how to interpret them. Thus, their own values often influence their interpretations, setting the stage for judicial restraint or judicial activism.

National Judicial Supremacy

The founders could not agree on the details concerning the structure of the federal judiciary. So after creating a single, Supreme Court, they left most of the details up to the First Congress. By the Judiciary Act of 1789, Congress established a system made up of district courts, circuit courts, and the Supreme Court.

Under Chief Justice John Marshall, the Supreme Court developed into a powerful branch of government that could check the power of other branches through its use of judicial review. In *Marbury* v. *Madison,* the Court for the first time declared a congressional statute unconstitutional. The Court thus established itself as the final authority on the meaning of the Constitution.

The Organization of the Courts

The U.S. court system is complex. In addition to a national system, separate court systems are operating in each state. The main entry points for cases into the national judicial system are the ninety-four federal district courts, which hear criminal cases involving violations of federal law, civil cases brought under federal law and in which the federal government is the plaintiff or defendant, and civil cases between citizens of different states when more than $75,000 is at issue. Federal courts handle far fewer cases than do state courts, but the number of cases in federal courts has grown and is generally related to the overall level of social, political, and economic activity in the nation.

Judges exert a policymaking function by applying rules (precedents) established in prior decisions (common or "judge-made" law) and by interpreting legislative acts (through a process of "statutory construction").

Appeals may be carried from federal district courts to one of the thirteen courts of appeals. Judges in the appeals courts sit in panels of three. They write and publish opinions on the cases they hear. These opinions establish legal precedents that serve as a basis for continuity and stability, following the principle of *stare decisis.*

Because relatively few cases are ever actually brought to the Supreme Court, the decision of a lower court is usually the final word. The decentralization of the system allows for individual judges in various district or circuit courts to interpret laws differently; this lack of uniformity may cause difficulties until, eventually, discrepancies are resolved by a Supreme Court decision.

The Supreme Court

The Supreme Court makes national policies—its decisions affect the nation as a whole. The Court's caseload includes a few cases that it hears as part of its original jurisdiction under the Constitution, but most cases come to the Court on appeal from lower courts or state courts.

The Court controls its docket and hears very few cases. Cases usually come to it only after all other avenues have been exhausted. Cases must also involve a substantial federal question. At least four justices must agree to hear a case, or it is not argued before the Court.

In deciding which cases to review, the Court often takes cues from the solicitor general, the Department of Justice official who represents the government before the Court. The solicitor general performs a dual role as an advocate for the president's policy preferences and as an officer of the Court, defending the institutional interests of the federal government.

After a case has been heard, the nine judges meet in conference to discuss their positions. A formal vote decides the outcome. As they approach cases, justices may differ in their view of their role. Some may practice judicial restraint, trying to stick closely to the intent of the legislators who made the law and to previous decisions of the courts. Other justices may take on the role of judicial activist, interpreting the law more loosely and in accord with their own policy preferences. Although justices may agree on what the particular result of a case should be, they may not agree fully on the legal reasons for the decision. In the Supreme Court's policymaking, both the Court's decision and the reasons offered for it are important. The opinion, or explanation of reasons for a decision, is critical. Sometimes, justices may shift their votes if they do not believe an opinion is based on legal reasoning they are able to support. Justices will also try to win the support of their fellow justices in conference and through their opinion writing.

The chief justice is particularly well placed to exercise leadership on the Court. He or she directs the conference and by tradition speaks first and votes last in court deliberations. When voting with the majority, the chief justice assigns the opinion. Astute use of these powers can make the chief justice an intellectual leader, a social leader, and a policy leader, although perhaps only Justice Marshall ever filled all three roles.

Judicial Recruitment

No formal constitutional requirements for federal judgeships exist, although a set of standards has evolved. By law, judges must be approved by the Senate. Over the years, an informal practice known as "senatorial courtesy" has given the senior senator of the president's party a substantial amount of control over judicial appointments in his state, although this power is not as extensive as it once was. In addition, the American Bar Association historically screened candidates and ranked them as qualified or unqualified for office, though the ABA is no longer part of the official recruitment process.

Presidents generally seek to appoint judges who share their ideological orientation.

The Consequences of Judicial Decisions

Only a small percentage of federal cases wind up in court. Many civil cases end in out-of-court settlements. In criminal cases, defendants often admit guilt and plea bargain.

Although the courts have the power to make judgments, they do not have the power to implement the policies they make. They must rely on the other branches of government for that. Judicial opinions are not always popular. Courts as institutions may appear to be countermajoritarian. Yet, Supreme Court decisions generally reflect majority sentiment. (Two major exceptions are the abortion issue, where the public is sharply divided, and school prayer, where the public opposes the Court's decisions.) Key reasons are that the Court tends to defer to the law, and the law tends to mirror public opinion. In addition, the Court moves closer to public opinion during times of crisis. Finally, rulings that reflect public opinion are less likely to be changed than are those that conflict with it.

The Courts and Models of Democracy

The major question in evaluating the role of the courts as creators of policy concerns how far judges stray from existing statutes and precedents. Majoritarians would want judges to cling closely to the letter of the law, leaving it to the elected legislature to decide how much emphasis to put on equality or order. Pluralists think the values of judges should come into play to advance the values and interests of the population. Several aspects of the judicial system contribute to making it conform to the pluralist model. Among these are the decentralized court system, which offers multiple access points to the legal system, and class-action suits, which allow individuals to pool their claims.

KEY TERMS

judicial review

criminal case

civil case

common (judge-made) law

U.S. district court

U.S. court of appeals

precedent

stare decisis

original jurisdiction

appellate jurisdiction

federal question

docket

rule of four

solicitor general

amicus curiae **brief**

judicial restraint

judicial activism

judgment

argument

concurrence

dissent

senatorial courtesy

plea bargain

class action

RESEARCH AND RESOURCES

An excellent starting point for research on the Supreme Court is *Congressional Quarterly*'s *Guide to the U.S. Supreme Court*, 4th ed. (Washington, D.C.: Congressional Quarterly Press, 2004). This hefty two-volume set contains an overview of the origins and development of the Court and detailed analyses of the role of the Court in the federal system, of Court decisions on individual rights, of pressures on the Court, and of the Court at work. Brief biographies of every justice who ever served on the Court and short summaries of major decisions are included.

What if you need more than a brief summary of a case—what if you must examine the actual opinion handed down by the Court? If it is a recent case, opinions are available online directly from the

Supreme Court the day they are announced at <http://www.supremecourtus.gov>. Several other strategies are open for you if you are looking for decisions that predate the decisions on the Court's website. For example, imagine you are looking for the Supreme Court decision that forced President Nixon to surrender the Watergate tapes. On the Internet, you can try "Findlaw: Internet Legal Resources" at <http://www.findlaw.com/>. Findlaw provides the text of Supreme Court and Circuit Court opinions back to 1893. "Oyez" at <http://www.oyez.org/> will provide access to the most important text and decisions, including audio recordings of oral arguments before the Court. The Legal Information Institute at Cornell University <http://www.law.cornell.edu/> has full texts of Court decisions available as soon as they are announced. If you are not able to access the Internet, you might consult the subject index at the back of *Guenther's United States Supreme Court Decisions*. Look up the word *Watergate* and you'll find a reference leading to the place where the case you want appears in the listing in the front of the book. When you track that reference down, you'll find the case cited as *United States* v. *Richard M. Nixon*, 418 US 683. This is the citation for the case as it appears in *U.S. Reports*, the official version of the opinion published by the U.S. Government Printing Office. The number preceding "US" indicates the volume number, while the number following "US" gives the page number where the case is to be found.

If you are working on a project that involves references to eighteenth- and nineteenth-century cases, you will sometimes find cases cited this way:

- *Calder* v. *Bull* (3 Dall. 386), 1798

- *Fletcher* v. *Peck* (6 Cr. 87), 1810

- *McCulloch* v. *Maryland* (4 Wheat. 316), 1819

Until 1875, the official reports of the Supreme Court were designated by the last name of the court reporter who recorded the decisions. The abbreviations in the above examples stand for the first three court reporters, whose names were Dallas, Cranch, and Wheaton. The citation for the *McCulloch* case tells you that it will be found in the fourth volume of Wheaton's reports, on page 316.

Here is a list of the early reporters, their dates of service, and the redesignations assigned to make each conform to the *U.S. Reports* system:

Early Designation		Abbr.	Dates Covered	U.S. Reports
1–4	Dallas	(Dall.)	(1790–1800)	1–4
1–9	Cranch	(Cr.)	(1801–1815)	5–13
1–12	Wheaton	(Wheat.)	(1816–1827)	14–25
1–16	Peters	(Pet.)	(1828–1842)	26–41
1–24	Howard	(How.)	(1843–1860)	42–65
1–2	Black	(Black)	(1861–1862)	66–67
1–23	Wallace	(Wall.)	(1863–1874)	68–90

To cite a case in a footnote or bibliography, you should include the official name of the case (usually the names of the two parties to the case), the volume of the report where the case appears (for example, Cr., Wall., U.S.), the page number where the decision may be found, and the year in which the case was decided.

The federal judiciary branch produces a wide range of publications in addition to the opinions delivered in specific cases. For reports on topics ranging from bankruptcy to the death penalty, see <http://www.uscourts.gov/publications.html>.

USING YOUR KNOWLEDGE

1. Using the procedures outlined in the Research and Resources section above, locate the cases popularly known as:

    *   the *Bakke* case

    *   the "Seven Dirty Words" case

    *   *Roe* v. *Wade*

    Find each opinion on the internet and print off the citation from the first page of the opinion.

2. Using the procedures outlined in the Research and Resources section above, locate cases dealing with each of these subjects:

    *   the Amish challenge to compulsory school attendance laws

    *   the 2000 presidential election

    *   draft card destruction

    *   professional football

    Give a full citation for each case.

GETTING INVOLVED

If you see yourself sitting on the Supreme Court some day, perhaps you'd like to try an internship while you are still in college. Most opportunities to work at the Supreme Court take the form of clerkships and are available only to recent law school graduates. However, a small number of highly competitive internships are available to undergraduates. Some background in constitutional law is usually expected. Internships are available summer, fall, and winter. They are unpaid, although a small scholarship may be available. For further information, see <http://www.supremecourtus.gov/jobs/jip/jip.html> or contact the Supreme Court of the United States, Judicial Internship Program, Office of the Administrative Assistant to the Chief Justice, Room 5, Washington, D.C. 20543. Telephone: (202) 479-3415.

SAMPLE EXAM QUESTIONS

Multiple-Choice Questions

1. When judges interject their own values into interpretation of cases, they are practicing
    a. liberalism.
    b. conservatism.
    c. judicial restraint.
    d. judicial activism.
2. The power to declare congressional acts invalid is called
    a. judicial review.
    b. judicial restraint.
    c. judicial activism.
    d. adjudication.
3. Judicial review of congressional legislation was first established in the case of
    a. *Marbury* v. *Madison.*
    b. *Fletcher* v. *Peck.*
    c. *McCulloch* v. *Maryland.*
    d. *Barron* v. *Baltimore.*

4. The Constitution created

    a. only the Supreme Court and established its original jurisdiction.
    b. only the Supreme Court and established its appellate jurisdiction.
    c. only the Supreme Court and established its size.
    d. the Supreme Court as well as the circuit courts of appeals and the district courts.

5. Federal district courts

    a. are the trial courts in the federal system.
    b. usually publish written opinions.
    c. hear all civil cases between citizens of different states.
    d. are the appeals court in the federal system.

6. Congress may change all of the following *except* the

    a. organization of district and circuit courts.
    b. Supreme Court's appellate jurisdiction.
    c. Supreme Court's original jurisdiction.
    d. number of justices on the Supreme Court.

7. U.S. circuit courts

    a. are the main trial courts of the system.
    b. are appellate courts.
    c. rarely issue written opinions.
    d. do not establish precedents.

8. The expression for the bias in favor of precedents or existing decisions is

    a. stare decisis.
    b. tort.
    c. amicus curiae.
    d. judicial review.

9. When a justice supports a judgment but disagrees with other justices about the reasons for deciding that way, he or she may write a separate opinion called a

    a. dissenting opinion.
    b. concurring opinion.
    c. writ of certiorari.
    d. unanimous opinion.

10. The official who represents the government before the Supreme Court is called the

    a. solicitor general.
    b. public defender.
    c. attorney general.
    d. amicus curiae.

11. Conservative justices such as Antonin Scalia and Clarence Thomas usually prefer

    a. freedom to equality and equality to order.
    b. order to freedom and freedom to equality.
    c. equality to freedom and freedom to order.
    d. equality to order and order to freedom.

12. Liberal justices such as Ruth Bader Ginsburg and John Paul Stevens usually prefer

    a. freedom to equality and equality to order.
    b. order to freedom and freedom to equality.
    c. equality to freedom and freedom to order.
    d. equality to order and order to freedom.

13. To win Senate confirmation, judicial nominees usually need
    a. to be political neutrals.
    b. to have support from the state's senior senator in the president's party.
    c. to practice judicial restraint.
    d. All of the above.

14. In making appointments to the federal judiciary, President Carter emphasized
    a. political ideology.
    b. racial and gender diversity.
    c. wealth.
    d. equality.

15. Most criminal cases
    a. end up in federal courts.
    b. wind up in the Supreme Court.
    c. end up with a plea bargain.
    d. are taken to trial.

16. A device for pooling the claims of similar individuals to try them in a single lawsuit is called a
    a. writ of certiorari.
    b. "friend of the court" brief.
    c. writ of mandamus.
    d. class-action suit.

17. Most cases reach the Supreme Court
    a. under its original jurisdiction.
    b. under its appellate jurisdiction.
    c. by means of certain automatic triggers.
    d. by vote of a majority of the justices.

18. Supreme Court decisions
    a. embody the principles of majoritarian government.
    b. are consistently out of step with public opinion.
    c. mirror public opinion on abortion and school prayer.
    d. are surprisingly consistent with public opinion.

19. Which of the following is *not* a component of judicial review as established in *Marbury* v. *Madison* and other early Supreme Court cases?
    a. Courts may declare federal, state, or local laws invalid.
    b. Federal laws and treaties take precedence over state or local laws when there is a conflict.
    c. The Supreme Court is the final authority on the meaning of the Constitution.
    d. State courts are obliged to follow the federal Constitution only as it is interpreted by their state constitutions.

20. Maintaining public order through criminal law is mainly a function of the
    a. national government.
    b. national and state governments.
    c. state governments.
    d. state and local governments.

Essay Questions

1. Distinguish between judicial restraint and judicial activism. Is there a necessary connection between restraint and activism, on the one hand, and political ideology, on the other?

2. What is "judicial review"? Explain how it was established in *Marbury* v. *Madison*.

3.   Describe the main differences between federal district courts and U.S. circuit courts.

4.   Discuss ways in which a chief justice may exert leadership on the Supreme Court. Give concrete examples to illustrate your answer.

5.   Explain the process through which individuals become federal judges.

ANSWERS TO MULTIPLE-CHOICE QUESTIONS

1.   d
2.   a
3.   a
4.   a
5.   a
6.   c
7.   b
8.   a
9.   b
10. a
11. b
12. c
13. b
14. b
15. c
16. d
17. b
18. d
19. d
20. d

CHAPTER 12

Order and Civil Liberties

LEARNING OBJECTIVES

After reading this chapter you should be able to

- Define the key terms identified in the chapter margins.

- Distinguish between civil rights and civil liberties.

- Explain how the establishment clause of the First Amendment has been interpreted in cases involving government aid to church-related schools and prayer in public schools.

- Describe the two approaches developed by the Supreme Court for dealing with cases involving the free-expression clause of the First Amendment.

- List the major exceptions to the First Amendment's protection of freedom of speech.

- Discuss prior restraint, libel, and censorship as possible limitations on freedom of the press in the United States.

- Explain how the Fourteenth Amendment has been used to extend the protections of the Bill of Rights to citizens in cases involving the states.

- Explain where the Supreme Court found the right to privacy in the Constitution and show how the right has been applied in cases involving abortion, birth control, and homosexuality.

ORDER AND CIVIL LIBERTIES AND THE CHALLENGE OF DEMOCRACY

Should students be able to wear T-shirts with any slogan, regardless of how controversial? Can school officials suppress student expression? This chapter looks at how the courts have resolved conflicts among the three values that are so important to democratic politics—order, freedom, and equality. Court decisions involve a balancing act among these values. A review of the cases in the chapter may lead a person to conclude that not one of these values is ever preferred unconditionally over the others. The freedoms of speech, press, and assembly are all particularly important to the conduct of democracy, yet the Supreme Court has sometimes limited them in the name of order when exercising these freedoms would create a very serious danger. Furthermore, where certain types of expression are concerned—for example, obscenity—the Court may choose to uphold the value of order by supporting community standards. On the other hand, the fact that the exercise of these freedoms may offer an affront to the majority and threaten to disrupt established patterns of social order is not always enough to convince the Court to restrict them.

As part of the task of upholding order, the government punishes those who violate laws and endanger the lives and property of others. Yet, those accused of crimes may not be deprived of their freedoms without due process of law. This means, among other things, that they must be informed of their legal rights, including the right to an attorney and to protection against self-incrimination. Enforcing these rights may sometimes mean that guilty people go free, but in balancing order and freedom, the courts often decide that the threat to order posed by freeing a guilty person is less worrisome than the threat to freedom posed by denying an accused person due process of law.

The Court often uses the Bill of Rights to protect citizens from the national government. But the Bill of Rights did not initially apply to the states; so while the national government was barred, for example, from using illegally obtained evidence in trials, state courts were not. Gradually in this century, however, the Court has used the Fourteenth Amendment to extend the provisions of the Bill of Rights to the states as well.

CHAPTER OVERVIEW

The Bill of Rights

In the U.S. system, the values of freedom, equality, and order often conflict. When Brett Barber was told to change his shirt or leave school, his freedom came into conflict with the community's demand for order. In such a case, each side may claim that its view is rooted in the law. Disputes over issues involving such basic values are usually settled in the courts by our unelected judiciary. Conflicts often arise from different views on the rights of citizens, and a major source of people's rights is the Constitution—in the Bill of Rights and the Fourteenth Amendment. The Constitution guarantees civil rights and civil liberties. A civil right declares what the government must do or provide; a civil liberty is a guarantee to individual citizens that acts as a restraint on government.

Freedom of Religion

The First Amendment provides for freedom of religion, speech, press, and assembly. These protections of individual freedoms may conflict with the need for order—an example of the original dilemma of government discussed in Chapter 1. Freedom of religion is guaranteed in two clauses. The first, the establishment clause, forbids any law that would create an official religion; the second, the free-exercise clause, prevents the government from interfering with the practice of religion. The establishment clause erected "a wall of separation between church and state." The government is also supposed to be neutral between religions and between the religious and the nonreligious. On certain issues, such as government aid to church-related schools, the Supreme Court has allowed what opponents have seen as violations of the establishment clause. Reasoning that textbook loans and transportation are aids to students, not churches, the Court has allowed some support to church schools. In 1971, the *Lemon* test put forth guidelines for determining constitutionality under the establishment clause. On the issue of school prayer, however, the Court has maintained a consistent position that officially sanctioned public school prayer violates the establishment clause. However, student religious groups may not be prohibited from using school facilities if the same facilities are available to other student groups. This principle of neutrality has taken on great significance in recent years, partially eclipsing the "wall of separation" metaphor.

The free-exercise clause also gives rise to conflicts when the practice of a certain religion leads a person to do what is forbidden by law or to refuse to do what is required by law. A person may not be forced to take a job that requires him or her to work on the Sabbath, but the Court has forbidden participation in traditional religious rituals that involve the use of illegal drugs. The Court reasoned that religious beliefs are inviolate, but antisocial actions in the name of religion are not protected by the Constitution. Here again, the Court raised the theme of neutrality, arguing that otherwise valid laws regarding drug use (or, in a later case, zoning) apply to religious as well as secular institutions. Neutral laws that indirectly restrict religious practices are acceptable; only laws aimed at religious groups are constitutionally prohibited. The perceived narrowing of the range of free expression of religion led Congress to pass the Religious Freedom Restoration Act. However, the Court declared that law unconstitutional in 1997.

Freedom of Expression

Freedom of expression, including freedom of speech and freedom of the press, provide a right to unrestricted discussion of public affairs, yet these rights have never been absolute. Initially, the First Amendment clauses seemed aimed at preventing prior restraint. As the First Amendment speech doctrines developed, justices argued that speech creating a "clear and present danger" may be limited. "Symbolic speech" may receive even less protection, although the Supreme Court has ruled that flag burning is a constitutionally protected form of expression. Obscenity—although hard to define—is not protected by the Constitution, and the government may regulate distribution of obscene materials. However, attempts to regulate the distribution of sexual materials to minors over the Internet have run repeatedly into free expression hurdles.

Freedom of the press, including the ability to collect and report information without government interference, is crucial in a free society. Print media defend this freedom as absolute, although electronic media have had to accept some government regulation. Individuals may sue the media for libel, but public figures must show that the statements were made with knowledge that they were false or with reckless disregard for their truth or falsity in order to win a libel suit. Basically, freedom of the press means freedom from prior restraint. The Court has been reluctant to limit freedom of the press to ensure a fair trial. Yet, reporters are not protected from the demands of law enforcement and may be required to reveal their sources.

The First Amendment also provides the right to peaceably assemble and to petition the government for redress of grievances. This right has merged with freedom of speech and freedom of the press under the general heading of freedom of expression.

The Right to Bear Arms

The Second Amendment's guarantee of the right to keep and bear arms is a source of great controversy. Advocates of gun control see the guarantee as a collective one, centered on the right of states to maintain militias. Opponents of gun control argue that this amendment protects the individual's right to own guns.

Applying the Bill of Rights to the States

The Bill of Rights was created to put limits on the power of the national government. Initially, its provisions did not apply to states. Under the Fourteenth Amendment, however, nearly all of the Bill of Rights has gradually been extended to all levels of government. The Fourteenth Amendment guarantees people due process of law. The Court has interpreted this provision to mean that, in criminal proceedings, defendants in both state and national cases must be told about their constitutional rights, including their right to remain silent and their right to an attorney. The Court still allows jury size in trials to vary from state to state, however. The right to an attorney is considered fundamental, while the right to trial by a jury of a certain size is not. The Fourth Amendment provides people with freedom from unreasonable searches and seizures. The exclusionary rule, which disallows the use of evidence obtained illegally, helps to ensure this right, although this rule has been weakened in recent years. Interpretation of the exclusionary rule continues to divide the Court and serves as an example of the conflict between freedom and order.

The Ninth Amendment and Personal Autonomy

The Ninth Amendment left open the possibility that there were other rights, not enumerated, which might also be free from government interference. In the 1960s and 1970s, the Supreme Court used the Ninth Amendment as the basis for asserting that people have a right to privacy and that that right allows individuals to make their own choices about birth control and abortion. In addition, in *Lawrence and*

Garner v. *Texas*, the Court extended the right of privacy to cover private homosexual acts between consenting adults.

KEY TERMS AND CASES

Terms
civil liberties

civil rights

establishment clause

free-exercise clause

strict scrutiny

free-expression clauses

prior restraint

clear and present danger test

public figures

bill of attainder

ex post facto law

obligation of contracts

Miranda **warning**

exclusionary rule

good faith exception

Cases
Lemon v. *Kurtzman*

Zelman v. *Simmons-Haris*

Engel v. *Vitale*

Sherbert v. *Verner*

Brandenburg v. *Ohio*

Tinker v. *Des Moines Independent County School District*

Miller v. *California*

Reno v. *ACLU*

New York Times v. *Sullivan*

New York Times v. *United States*

Palko v. *Connecticut*

Gideon v. *Wainwright*

Griswold v. *Connecticut*

Roe v. *Wade*

Lawrence and Garner v. *Texas*

RESEARCH AND RESOURCES

This chapter deals mostly with the protection and extension of civil liberties as a result of Supreme Court decisions. The text describes the Court's discovery of a right to privacy. In the 1970s, Congress also took some measures to protect two individual rights not explicitly specified in the Constitution, namely, the right to privacy and the right to information. Congress passed a pair of acts known as the Privacy Act and the Freedom of Information Act. The first of these grants all individuals access to information the government keeps about them; the second gives people a right to see much of the information collected by the government. This section of the study guide outlines methods for using the Freedom of Information Act.

The government collects information on practically everything, and much of that material is in file drawers and computers in Washington rather than publicly disseminated in the form of published government documents. How do you get information that is gathered, but not published, by the government? What rights do you have to it?

Answers to these questions are found in the Freedom of Information Act (FOIA). The FOIA, first passed in 1966, marked a revolution in government record handling. The act shifted the burden of proof. Formerly, the person requesting information had been required to convince the government that the material should be provided; now the government must provide information unless it can give a specific reason under the statute why the information should be denied.

The FOIA applies to information held by the administrative agencies of the government (including the executive office of the president), but it does not apply to records held by Congress, the courts, or state governments (almost every state has its own act governing availability of public records). In 1974, the FOIA was amended, speeding and easing the process of gaining access to records.

What sort of information might you find under the FOIA? Here are some examples:

- Reports on federally supported nursing homes (Department of Health and Human Services)

- Records of regulatory agencies concerning pollution control programs (Environmental Protection Agency)

- Test results on the efficacy of drugs (Food and Drug Administration)

- Consumer complaints registered with the Fair Trade Commission

Under statute, nine categories of information may be denied to you, including agency personnel records; material on criminal investigations that might be an invasion of personal privacy, deprive a person of the right to a fair trial, or compromise a confidential source; and properly classified national defense or foreign policy secrets.

To obtain information under the FOIA, you must decide what information you want and which agency has it. You do not have to specify a document by its exact name or title, but you must provide a reasonable description of the information you are seeking. You might begin by looking at the *United States Government Manual* to find the agency that seems most likely to have the kind of information you want. Next, check the *Federal Register,* which lists descriptions of all the record systems kept by the government (including those to which you may be denied access), to find out if the agency keeps the records you want. The better able you are to identify the material you want, the more likely you are to receive it quickly. If your request is clear and specific, you may also reduce the search fees the agency may charge. Under the law, the government is allowed to charge you for searching for the material (anywhere from $10–$60 an hour depending upon the agency and the level of employee required to conduct the search) and for photocopying (generally $0.15 a page).

The Department of Justice hosts a FOIA site that includes both FOIA links and contact information for the major executive branch departments and agencies. The DOJ site is available at <http://www.usdoj.gov/04foia/index.html>. Also, see the Electronic Privacy Information Center, which maintains an extensive list of resources, including more information about the FOIA, at <http://epic.org/open_gov/>. Another useful resource is the Federation of American Scientists' Project on Government Secrecy site at <http://www.fas.org/sgp/index.html>. This site points out many of the challenges in successfully using the FOIA.

USING YOUR KNOWLEDGE

1. Follow the process outlined in the Research and Resources section and prepare a request for information obtainable under the Freedom of Information Act.

2. Visit the FBI's electronic reading room at <http://foia.fbi.gov/room.htm> and browse the files for well-known people such as Mickey Mantle, Elvis Presley, and Jackie Robinson. What kinds of information were collected?

SAMPLE EXAM QUESTIONS

Multiple-Choice Questions

1. The Bill of Rights was proposed

    a. as a means of eliminating opposition to the Constitution.
    b. by antifederalists as a means of scuttling the Constitution.
    c. as an integral part of the Constitution.
    d. as a necessary limit on the power of state governments.

2. The establishment clause of the First Amendment

    a. establishes the United States as a Christian nation.
    b. forbids the establishment of an official religion.
    c. has been used by the Supreme Court to justify the practice of prayer in public schools.
    d. has outlawed any government funding for education in church schools.

3. The three-pronged test to determine whether aid to church schools is constitutional is called the

    a. *Lemon* test.
    b. *Miranda* test.
    c. clear and present danger test.
    d. *Engle* test.

4. Which of the following questions is *not* part of the traditional test applied to determine whether a law providing for government aid to church schools is constitutional?

    a. Does it have a secular purpose?
    b. Does it advance or inhibit religion?
    c. Is it required by a federal law, such as the Americans with Disabilities Act?
    d. Does it entangle the government excessively with religion?

5. The free-exercise clause of the First Amendment

    a. permits all beliefs and practices of all religions.
    b. permits all beliefs but allows for limitation of some religious practices.
    c. may, in rare cases, allow the government to compel belief.
    d. protects beliefs and practices of Christianity only.

6. The press clause has been most effective in prohibiting

    a. prior restraint on publications.
    b. libel suits for works published.
    c. requirements that news reporters reveal their sources.

    d.   regulation of obscene publications.

7.   Under the First Amendment, freedom of speech

    a.   is absolute.

    b.   extends equally to verbal and symbolic or nonverbal expression.

    c.   may be limited when a speech is designed to provoke lawless action and has a high probability of doing so.

    d.   is prohibited to communists or members of the Ku Klux Klan.

8.   In *Miller* v. *California*, the Supreme Court

    a.   rejected all regulation of obscene material.

    b.   decided that works violating community standards might be declared obscene.

    c.   abandoned all attempts to provide a standard for obscenity.

    d.   replaced state determinations of obscenity with a national standard.

9.   The right to keep and bear arms

    a.   is linked in the Constitution to the need for a well-regulated militia.

    b.   entitles citizens to own any type of weapon.

    c.   may not be subject to state or federal licensing restrictions.

    d.   All of the above.

10.   The protections of the Bill of Rights have gradually been extended to the states through

    a.   the Fourteenth Amendment.

    b.   the *Slaughterhouse* cases.

    c.   *Barron* v. *Baltimore*.

    d.   the privileges and immunities clause.

11.   The Sixth Amendment provision for a right to counsel was extended to the states in

    a.   *Palko* v. *Connecticut*.

    b.   *Near* v. *Minnesota*.

    c.   *Gideon* v. *Wainwright*.

    d.   *Miranda* v. *Arizona*.

12.   The *Miranda* warning

    a.   protects against illegal search and seizure.

    b.   informs suspects of their right to remain silent and to be represented by an attorney.

    c.   informs suspects of their right to a trial by a twelve-person jury.

    d.   protects suspects against being placed in double jeopardy.

13.   The main source used by the Supreme Court to justify introducing an unenumerated right of privacy was the

    a.   Fourteenth Amendment.

    b.   Ninth Amendment.

    c.   Sixth Amendment.

    d.   Second Amendment.

14.   In *Roe* v. *Wade*, the Supreme Court

    a.   upheld order over freedom.

    b.   rejected all state regulation of abortion.

    c.   left decisions on abortion up to a mother and her physician during the first three months of pregnancy.

    d.   permanently settled the abortion question.

15.   Symbolic expression

    a.   generally receives less protection than pure speech.

    b.   generally receives more protection than pure speech.

    c.   generally receives the same protection as pure speech.

    d.   does not have any connection to the First Amendment.

16. The clear and present danger test
    a. was originally enunciated by Justice Holmes in the *Gitlow* case.
    b. distinguishes the advocacy of ideas from the incitement to disorder.
    c. was first applied by Jefferson to the Alien and Sedition Acts.
    d. applies not only to speech but to symbolic expression and matters of personal appearance as well.

17. In *New York Times* v. *United States*, the opinion of the Supreme Court
    a. upheld the government's right to halt publication of the Pentagon Papers.
    b. upheld press freedom from prior restraint as an absolute.
    c. found that the government had not shown that immediate, inevitable, and irreparable harm would follow publication of the Pentagon Papers.
    d. argued that publication of the Pentagon Papers would prolong the war and embarrass the government.

18. The exclusionary rule is used to prohibit
    a. federal funds from being used to support religious schools.
    b. foreigners from entering the United States.
    c. illegally obtained evidence from being used in criminal prosecutions.
    d. publication of slanderous or libelous materials.

19. If high school students wished to meet on school property in an after-school Bible study group, they would be
    a. permitted to meet if students from other organizations were also permitted to meet on school property after school.
    b. denied access because of Supreme Court rulings based on the establishment clause.
    c. denied access because prayer in the schools is unconstitutional.
    d. permitted to meet only if students from all other religions also organized groups.

20. Before the Fourteenth Amendment was passed and applied to the states, the Constitution still barred both state and national governments from
    a. passing ex post facto laws.
    b. establishing an official religion.
    c. denying citizens the right to a jury trial.
    d. searching property without warrants.

Essay Questions

1. What conflicts arise between the values of freedom, order, and equality when a public school district attempts to regulate what messages can be worn on a T-shirt at school?

2. While the First Amendment protects speech, the protection is not unlimited. Describe the limits on free speech that the Supreme Court has defined and explain the Court's reasoning.

3. Explain the tension between the free-exercise clause and the establishment clause. How has the Supreme Court's view of the establishment clause changed over the last century?

4. How has the Supreme Court applied the Bill of Rights to the states at different times in American history?

5. How does the Supreme Court's changing position on the issue of abortion illustrate an evolving balance between freedom and order?

ANSWERS TO MULTIPLE-CHOICE QUESTIONS

1. a
2. b
3. a
4. c
5. b
6. a
7. c
8. b
9. a
10. a
11. c
12. b
13. b
14. c
15. a
16. b
17. c
18. c
19. a
20. a

CHAPTER 13

Equality and Civil Rights

LEARNING OBJECTIVES

After reading this chapter you should be able to

- Define the key terms identified in the chapter margins.

- Explain why the Civil War amendments proved ineffective in ensuring racial equality.

- Distinguish between *de jure* and *de facto* segregation.

- Describe the tactics of the civil rights movement and the passage of the 1964 Civil Rights Act.

- Contrast the key civil rights issues facing African Americans with those facing Native Americans, Hispanic Americans, and disabled Americans.

- List the major legislative and judicial milestones in the struggle for equal rights for women.

- Discuss how affirmative action programs have led to charges of reverse discrimination.

- Distinguish between equality of opportunity and equality of outcome.

EQUALITY AND CIVIL RIGHTS AND THE CHALLENGE OF DEMOCRACY

As the chapter indicates, the national government has not always prized equality so highly. Throughout most of U.S. history, disadvantaged groups have struggled to achieve political and social equality. Much of the time, the national government supported the freedom of states and individuals to discriminate and treat people differently on the basis of their race, sex, or other characteristics. Thus, states were free to design voting requirements in a way that included only white males. Blacks and whites could be educated at segregated schools. Individuals could refuse to serve blacks at lunch counters.

Over the past few decades, however, the government's priorities shifted. With the separate-but-equal decision in *Plessy* v. *Ferguson* in 1896, the national government tried to sweep under the rug the conflict between equality and freedom. By announcing in *Brown* v. *Board of Education* in 1954 that "separate is inherently unequal," the national government faced the tension between freedom and equality and the fact that more of one usually means less of the other. The meaning of equality also creates difficulties. Many who may agree on the need for equality of opportunity will not support measures they think are geared to produce equality of outcome.

The struggle for civil rights also illustrates the conflict between pluralism and majoritarianism. In accepting the demands of black citizens, the national government acts in a way that is more pluralist than majoritarian. As Chapter 1 pointed out, majoritarian democracy does what the majority wants and thus may allow discrimination against minorities, even though the substantive outcome (inequality) seems undemocratic.

Thus, questions about what kind of public policies should be adopted to achieve equality are often highly controversial. If the nation wants to promote racial and gender equality among doctors or sheet-metal workers, for example, it may design policies to help previously disadvantaged and underrepresented groups gain jobs in these areas. This practice, however, may lead to charges of reverse discrimination.

Blacks seeking civil rights not only had to contend with being members of a minority group, but they also were largely excluded from the electoral process. Under the leadership of the National Association for the Advancement of Colored People (NAACP), they adopted the strategies of lobbying legislators and pressing claims before the judiciary, the branch of government least susceptible to majoritarian influences. Later, as the civil rights movement grew (and as majority opinion became more accepting of the cause), they emphasized the importance of legislation as a method of achieving equality and also used the techniques of civil disobedience to challenge laws they believed to be unjust.

The women's movement offers an interesting contrast. Women are not actually a minority group; they are a majority of the population. Yet, in the struggle to pass the Equal Rights Amendment (ERA), pluralism prevailed when the amendment failed. The amending process, by requiring extraordinary majorities, gives enormous power to minorities bent on thwarting a particular cause.

CHAPTER OVERVIEW

Two Conceptions of Equality

Throughout much of U.S. history, civil rights—the powers and privileges supposedly guaranteed to individuals and protected from arbitrary removal at the hand of government—have often been denied to certain citizens on the basis of their race or sex. The pursuit of civil rights in the United States has been a story of the search for social and economic equality. But people differ on what equality means. Most Americans support equal opportunity, but many are less committed to equality of outcome.

The Civil War Amendments

After the Civil War, the Thirteenth, Fourteenth, and Fifteenth amendments were passed to ensure freedom and equality for black Americans. In addition, Congress passed civil rights acts in 1866 and 1875 to guarantee civil rights and access to public accommodations. While the legislative branch was attempting to strengthen black civil rights, the judicial branch weakened some of them through a number of decisions that gave states room to maneuver around civil rights laws. States responded with various measures limiting the rights of blacks, including poll taxes, grandfather clauses that prevented them from voting, and Jim Crow laws that restricted their use of public facilities. These restrictions were upheld in *Plessy* v. *Ferguson,* which justified them under the separate-but-equal doctrine. By the end of the nineteenth century, segregation was firmly and legally entrenched in the South.

The Dismantling of School Segregation

The NAACP led the campaign for black civil rights. Its activists used the mechanism of the courts to press for equal facilities for blacks and then to challenge the constitutionality of the separate-but-equal doctrine itself. In 1954, in *Brown* v. *Board of Education,* a class-action suit, the Supreme Court reversed its earlier decision in the *Plessy* case. It ruled that "separate educational facilities are inherently unequal" and that segregated schools must be integrated "with all deliberate speed" under the direction of the federal courts. The Court thus ordered an end to school segregation that had been imposed by law (*de jure* segregation). But in many parts of the country, segregation persisted because blacks and whites lived in different areas and sent their children to local schools (*de facto* segregation). This problem led the courts to require several remedies to achieve integration, including busing, racial quotas, and the pairing of noncontiguous school zones.

The Civil Rights Movement

The NAACP's use of the legal system ended school segregation and achieved some other more limited goals, but additional pressure for desegregation in all aspects of American life grew out of the civil rights movement. An early salvo in the civil rights movement came when blacks in Montgomery, Alabama, boycotted the city's bus system to protest Rosa Parks's arrest and the law that prohibited blacks from sitting in the front of buses. Under the leadership of Martin Luther King, Jr., the movement grew, and civil rights activities, including nonviolent civil disobedience, spread.

In the early 1960s, President Kennedy was gradually won over to supporting the civil rights movement. In 1963, he asked Congress to outlaw segregation in public accommodations. President Lyndon Johnson made passage of the Civil Rights Act of 1964 his top legislative priority, and the bill passed a few months after he assumed office. More civil rights legislation followed in 1965 and 1968. This time, the legality of civil rights acts was upheld by the Supreme Court.

Having civil rights laws on the books does not mean an end to discrimination once and for all, however. The Court, with a new conservative majority in the ascendancy, continued to issue decisions limiting the scope of previous civil rights rulings. Congress sought to restore rights previously recognized through the Civil Rights Act of 1991.

Civil Rights for Other Minorities

Civil rights legislation won through blacks' struggles also protects other minorities. Native Americans, Hispanic Americans, and disabled Americans were also often victims of discrimination. The Indian reservations established by the U.S. government were poverty-stricken. In the late 1960s and early 1970s, the frustrations of Native Americans erupted into militancy. By the mid-1970s and early 1980s, they began to win important legal victories, including compensation for land taken by the U.S. government. Recently, new entrepreneurial tribal leadership of Indian tribes has capitalized on the special status of their tribes and enjoyed economic success by sponsoring casino gambling ventures, though poverty is still widespread.

Hispanics who migrated to the United States seeking economic opportunities in the early Twentieth Century generally found poverty and discrimination instead. Approximately one-third of them returned to Mexico during the Great Depression. The Hispanic population in the United States has grown again since World War II and in 2003 became the single largest minority group in the United States. With this growth, Hispanics have become more successful in obtaining elected and appointed political offices.

Building on the model of existing civil rights laws, disabled Americans gained recognition as an oppressed minority and, through the 1990 Americans with Disabilities Act, received the protection of a right of access to employment and facilities.

Gender and Equal Rights: The Women's Movement

Civil rights have long been denied to women, partly as a result of policies designed to protect women from ill treatment. The Supreme Court upheld such protective legislation as being consistent with the "proper" role of women. Only after a long struggle did women win the right to vote under the Nineteenth Amendment, passed in 1920. But gaining the vote did not automatically bring equality for women. Discrimination continued in the workplace and elsewhere. It took legislation such as the 1964 Civil Rights Act and other legislation to prohibit some of the other forms of discrimination against women. In the early 1970s, the Court began to strike down gender-based discriminations that could not be justified as serving an important government purpose. In 1996, the Court applied a new standard of "skeptical scrutiny" to acts denying rights based on sex. This new standard makes distinctions based on sex almost as suspect as those based on race.

For many years, the Court proved reluctant to use the Fourteenth Amendment as the basis for guaranteeing women's rights. As a result, proponents of equal rights for women sought an amendment to ensure that women's rights stood on a clear constitutional footing. Although the ERA was ratified by thirty-five states, it fell three states short of the minimum required for adoption and did not become the law of the land.

Affirmative Action: Equal Opportunity or Equal Outcome?

The Johnson administration started several programs to overcome the effects of past discrimination by extending opportunities to groups previously denied rights. These affirmative action programs involved positive or active steps taken to assist members of groups formerly denied equality of opportunity.

These programs soon led to charges of reverse discrimination. The Court, however, has found some role for affirmative action programs. In the *Bakke* decision, a split court held that race could be one of several constitutionally permissible admissions criteria. In 2003 the Supreme Court reaffirmed its view that race could be taken into account in admitting students to higher education. Clarifying its earlier decisions, the Court indicated that if there is a compelling interest to consider race, it must be considered on an individual basis in the context of other factors.

KEY TERMS AND CASES

Terms

equality of opportunity

equality of outcome

invidious discrimination

civil rights

racism

poll tax

racial segregation

separate-but-equal doctrine

desegregation

de jure **segregation**

de facto **segregation**

civil rights movement

boycott

civil disobedience

protectionism

Nineteenth Amendment

sexism

Equal Rights Amendment (ERA)

affirmative action

Cases

Plessy v. *Ferguson*

Brown v. *Board of Education*

Brown v. *Board of Education II*

United States v. *Virginia*

Regents of the University of California v. *Bakke*

Gratz v. *Bollinger*

Grutter v. *Bollinger*

RESEARCH AND RESOURCES

Chapter 11 in this study guide explained how to find a Supreme Court opinion. Once you've located an opinion, however, you might still have some difficulty figuring out how to read it. Cases are reported beginning with a heading that gives the parties to the case, the docket number, the dates the argument was heard, and the date the decision was handed down. Next, in rather small print, comes the syllabus, which includes a summary of the facts of the case and the legal questions it raised, as well as a summary of what the Court decided, or held, in the case. The syllabus then identifies (1) the author of the Court's opinion, (2) the justices who joined in that opinion, (3) those who concurred with it, and (4) those who dissented.

Justices concur when they vote with the majority on the actual decision but do not fully agree with the reasoning behind the majority's decision. Justices in this position often write separate opinions detailing their differences with the opinion of the Court and outlining their reasoning. Justices who are in the minority may choose to write dissenting opinions explaining the reasons for their disagreement with the majority. Writers of concurring and dissenting opinions hope that their views might influence and persuade Court members in future decisions.

After the syllabus comes the full text of the opinion of the Court (in larger type). The opinion of the Court ends with the judgment—for example, "affirmed" or "denied." This is followed by the full text of any concurring opinions, followed by any dissenting opinions.

USING YOUR KNOWLEDGE

1. Visit <http://www.indiantrust.com> to get an unusual degree of insight into an important lawsuit regarding the national government's obligations to Native Americans. What are the plaintiffs accusing the government of doing or failing to do? What do the plaintiffs seek in their lawsuit? How has the government responded to these claims?

2. Select three of the cases discussed in this chapter of the text. Look them up in *U.S. Reports* or find them on-line. (Try <http://www.law.cornell.edu> and navigate from there to the particular case in which you are interested. Check under "historic" and "recent" decisions.) For each case, note the vote tally, who authored the opinion of the Court, which justices joined in that opinion, which ones wrote concurring opinions, and which ones wrote dissents.

SAMPLE EXAM QUESTIONS

Multiple-Choice Questions

1. The U.S. State Department's involvement in assessing racial discrimination stems primarily from

    a. the election of George W. Bush.
    b. localism.
    c. globalism.
    d. diversity.

2. Racial quotas and goals are most frequently connected to

    a. equality of incorporation.
    b. equality of opportunity.
    c. equality of outcome.
    d. equality of efficiency.

3. The Civil War amendments were adopted to

    a. provide freedom and equality for black Americans.
    b. redistrict congressional districts in the South.
    c. desegregate schools.
    d. establish uniform voting rights for minorities and women.

4. Which of the following was *not* a method used to keep African Americans from voting?

    a. Literacy tests
    b. Poll taxes
    c. Minimum education requirements
    d. Separate-but-equal elections

5. The Court decision that upheld separate-but-equal facilities for African Americans and whites was

    a. *Sweatt* v. *Painter*.
    b. *Plessy* v. *Ferguson*.
    c. *Brown* v. *Board of Education*.
    d. *United States* v. *Virginia*.

6. According to the text, Jim Crow laws proliferated after

    a. 1835.
    b. the Supreme Court struck down the Civil Rights Act of 1875.
    c. World War II.
    d. *Brown* v. *Board of Education*.

7. President Harry Truman took an important step toward racial equality when he ordered the desegregation of

    a. the Cabinet.
    b. the armed forces.
    c. public schools.
    d. the Democratic Club of Washington.

8. The most successful tactic used by the NAACP in its struggle to dismantle school segregation was

    a. boycotting.
    b. rioting.
    c. legal challenges.
    d. voter registration drives.

9. School segregation that results from racial patterns depending on where people happen to live is called

    a.   government-imposed segregation.
    b.   separate-but-equal facilities.
    c.   *de facto* segregation.
    d.   *de jure* segregation.

10. The Civil Rights Act of 1964

    a.   forbade employment discrimination against women among other things.
    b.   protects only African Americans.
    c.   made relatively few changes to the status quo.
    d.   was declared unconstitutional in *Adarand Constructors* v. *Peña*.

11. The Voting Rights Act of 1965 has been credited with

    a.   decreasing membership in the Ku Klux Klan by 45 percent.
    b.   banning the poll tax.
    c.   expanding the franchise to women.
    d.   doubling black voter registration in the South in only five years.

12. In a U.S. presidential election, Native Americans

    a.   cannot vote; as members of sovereign nations they do not have U.S. citizenship.
    b.   cannot vote; U.S. citizenship rights were exchanged for mineral royalties in 1936.
    c.   can vote; they were granted U.S. citizenship with the establishment of reservations.
    d.   can vote; they received U.S. citizenship in 1924.

13. Women were guaranteed the right to vote in state and national elections in the

    a.   Fourteenth Amendment.
    b.   Fifteenth Amendment.
    c.   Nineteenth Amendment.
    d.   Twenty-Second Amendment.

14. Until the 1970s, most laws affecting the civil rights of women were based on the principle of

    a.   equality.
    b.   freedom.
    c.   protectionism.
    d.   the ERA.

15. In *United States* v. *Virginia*, the Supreme Court ruled that official acts denying individuals rights or responsibilities based on their sex

    a.   are always unconstitutional.
    b.   face a "skeptical scrutiny" test.
    c.   are constitutional if the public approves.
    d.   require judicial approval prior to implementation.

16. The failure of the Equal Rights Amendment is an example of

    a.   the majoritarian theory of democracy.
    b.   a rejection of minority rights.
    c.   the triumph of equality over freedom.
    d.   the power of committed minorities in a pluralist system.

17. The *Bakke* decision suggested that affirmative action programs in education

    a.   were unconstitutional.
    b.   were constitutional if all races benefited equally by the programs.
    c.   could not take an applicant's race into consideration in admissions decisions.
    d.   could use race as a plus factor, but not as the deciding factor in admissions.

18. Supreme Court decisions in the 1990s
    a. consistently supported affirmative action quota systems.
    b. challenged equality of outcome systems.
    c. supported equality of outcome systems.
    d. ruled affirmative action unconstitutional.

19. American public opinion on affirmative action
    a. differs dramatically by the race of the respondent.
    b. is overwhelmingly negative.
    c. is overwhelmingly positive.
    d. is evenly split.

20. The controversy over affirmative action programs illustrates the tension between
    a. ethnicity and freedom.
    b. equality and order.
    c. freedom and order.
    d. freedom and equality.

Essay Questions

1. Discuss the significance of *Brown* v. *Board of Education*. How did this case fit into the broader struggle for racial equality?

2. Compare the struggles that women, African Americans, and Hispanics have faced in the United States in their attempts to secure political rights and economic equality.

3. What is meant by affirmative action? Explain the significance of the *Bakke* case to the application of affirmative action policies.

4. Distinguish between "equality of opportunity" and "equality of outcome." Which is more controversial? Why?

5. The Thirteenth, Fourteenth, and Fifteenth amendments were passed to guarantee political rights for African Americans. Explain why they were unsuccessful for so long in achieving this result.

ANSWERS TO MULTIPLE-CHOICE QUESTIONS

1. c
2. c
3. a
4. d
5. b
6. b
7. b
8. c
9. c
10. a
11. d
12. d
13. c
14. c
15. b
16. d
17. d
18. b
19. a
20. d

CHAPTER 14

Policymaking and the Budget

LEARNING OBJECTIVES

After reading this chapter you should be able to

- Define the key terms identified in the chapter margins.

- Explain the differences between distributive and redistributional policies.

- Describe the four main stages in the policymaking process.

- Explain the dynamics of issue network politics.

- Point out the differences between "iron triangles" and "issue networks."

- Compare and contrast monetary and fiscal policies with respect to the role of government in the economy.

- Outline the steps in the budgetary process.

- Show how the Gramm-Rudman Act represented a failure of the legislative and budgetary process.

- Explain the different effects that mandatory spending and discretionary spending have on the government's ability to balance the budget.

- Show how uncontrollable outlays limit possibilities for cutting the federal budget.

- List several possible objectives of tax policy.

- Indicate who pays for and who benefits from the social security system.

PUBLIC POLICY AND THE CHALLENGE OF DEMOCRACY

The government seeks to achieve its purposes by adopting plans of action, or policies. Government has several different and often-competing purposes, including maintaining order, promoting freedom, and enhancing equality. Different people inside and outside government attach different weight to these purposes, in general and often in specific cases as well. Given the multiplicity of actors, values, and interests involved in the political process, policymaking can be a complicated and sometimes contradictory business.

Policymaking in the U.S. system can be highly fragmented. Different organs of the national government often have overlapping jurisdictions or areas of responsibility. State governments, too, may develop policies. Coordinating a coherent policy is a challenge for actors in the legislative and executive branches.

People who make up issue networks concerned with specific areas of public policy bring enormous expertise to bear in public policy matters. Their activities fit well with a pluralist model of democracy, which promises considerable influence in the policy process to those with the greatest stake in an issue area. However, if pluralist politics is to be democratic, access must be open, and different interests must be able to compete on a relatively equal basis.

Making economic public policy, which includes making decisions about taxing and spending, is a value-laden political process. First of all, it involves making choices about the role of government. Should the government maintain more of a hands-off approach, or should it take a more active role?

Public economic policy also requires choices between equality and freedom. The structure of the taxing and spending policies themselves reveals a good bit about the public value system. Americans have moved away from progressive taxation, where the rich pay proportionately more, and the tax system serves as a means of redistributing wealth and promoting equality.

On the spending side, incremental budgeting processes have given rise to clientele groups that pressure Congress to keep their favorite programs alive. Other groups managed to get spending programs established firmly by law as entitlement programs.

Many federal aid programs are viewed as "entitlements," and aid recipients worked to protect the programs important to them. Older Americans of retirement age exercise enormous political power and are keenly interested in protecting the social security and Medicare programs.

CHAPTER OVERVIEW

Government Purposes and Public Policies

Governments attempt to achieve their purposes through public policies—that is, plans of action they adopt to solve social problems, counter threats, or use opportunities. Public policies are the means by which governments pursue certain goals in specific situations.

To analyze public policies, it helps to divide them into three categories—distributive policies that provide resources to a particular segment of the population, redistributional policies that transfer resources from one sector of society to another to promote equality, and regulatory policies that guide the operation of government programs and business markets.

Most policymaking processes include the following four stages:

- An agenda-setting stage, in which a problem is defined as a political problem

- A policy-formulation stage, in which possible solutions are developed in the form of policy proposals and decisions are made about which proposal (if any) to adopt

- An implementation stage, in which a policy is carried out (often amid difficulties in coordinating the activities of government officials at various levels who must implement the policy)

- A policy-evaluation stage, in which programs are analyzed to discover how well they work in practice

Evaluation results in feedback—that is, information that lets policymakers know how well programs are doing what they were created to do and whether they should be continued, expanded, changed, or cut. Feedback may lead to new items being put on the political agenda and, hence, to a new cycle of policymaking.

Fragmentation and Coordination

The policymaking process includes many actors pulling the process in different directions. The separation of powers creates tension between institutions, and the federal system includes multiple governments with sometimes incompatible interests. Yet even within one branch at one level of government, for example the national executive branch, agencies and departments find themselves competing for authority and resources. The president attempts to coordinate policy within his administration through the Office of Management and Budget, which reviews proposed legislation for consistency with the administration's goals. Reorganizing departments or agencies within the branch is another method presidents employ.

Outside of government, many interest groups try to influence policy in any given issue area. In Washington, U.S. government often amounts to "government by policy area," which involves interaction among various governmental institutions and private sector organizations. These actors, who share knowledge of and an interest in the particular policy under consideration, form an issue network.

In the past, political scientists often described policy areas as being dominated by "iron triangles"—tightly knit subsystems made up of the congressional committee leaders, key agency and bureau personnel, and top lobbyists concerned with a particular issue. More recently, the concept of "issue networks" has emerged to describe the policymaking process. Issue networks include a large and varied group of participants and are more easily penetrated than iron triangles (although they are still held together by technical mastery of particular policy areas). The rise of issue networks is caused in part by *institutional* fragmentation in the political system. Recall the proliferation of interest groups discussed in Chapter 7 and the decentralization of Congress discussed in Chapter 8. As a result, public policy may become more complex and unwieldy: as multiple parts of the government attack problems in different (and potentially conflicting) ways, we see *policy* fragmentation.

Although issue networks are more open than iron triangles, both fail to achieve the majoritarian vision of democratic government.

Economic Policy and the Budget

Taxing and spending are government's two major policy tools for influencing the economy. Their use depends on policymakers' beliefs about how the economy works and how much government should be involved in the economy. *Keynesian theory* relies on the government to deal with the problems of depression and inflation by adjusting fiscal policies (government taxing and spending) and monetary policy (the money supply).

Until 1921, the budget was the principal product of the many congressional committees charged with taxing and spending. The highly decentralized budgeting process was not well adapted to the needs of a growing industrial nation, however. A new process was devised in which the newly created Bureau of the Budget (later called the Office of Management and Budget, or OMB) helped the president submit budget proposals to Congress. This gave the president the opportunity to set the government's fiscal priorities.

The president's budget is the result of considerable politicking by departments and agencies. The current budgeting process is described as a creaky conglomeration of traditional procedures combined with structural reforms from the 1970s, external constraints from the 1980s, and changes under the 1990 Budget Enforcement Act. The two-step authorization and appropriation process divides budgeting responsibilities among several committees. This decentralization leaves many opportunities for interest groups to influence the process and makes it difficult to assign responsibilities for decisions on the budget as a whole.

Tax policy is designed to provide the money that government spends. Government may use tax policy to serve other purposes as well. Tax policy may be used as a method of making tax burdens more equitable or of introducing Keynesian controls on the economy. Tax reform in 1986 introduced a two-bracket tax system. Presidents Bush (the elder) and Clinton each added new brackets at the higher end of the income scale, thereby increasing the progressive nature of the tax system. The younger President Bush created a fifth tax bracket lowering taxes for some lower-income people. Changes in the economy have dramatic effects on tax revenues, and tax hikes or cuts appropriate under current conditions may not be optimal a few years later.

What does the government spend its money on? The largest expenditure goes to social security; next comes defense, followed by interest on the national debt. Government spending has increased from about 15 percent of gross domestic product after World War II to over 20 percent today. This increase is partly a result of incremental budgeting practices and uncontrollable outlays such as social security. Concern with the deficit has checked some incremental budgeting, but certain spending programs have remained largely uncontrollable. Programs such as social security and Medicare, in particular, are difficult to cut because they are legally mandated and backed by politically powerful interests, such as the elderly.

KEY TERMS

public policy

distributive policies

redistributional policies

regulation

agenda setting

policy formulation

implementation

policy evaluation

feedback

fragmentation

issue network

Keynesian theory

fiscal policies

monetary policies

inflation

deficit financing

Council of Economic Advisers (CEA)

Federal Reserve System

fiscal year (FY)

budget authority

budget outlays

receipts

national debt

Office of Management and Budget (OMB)

tax committees

authorization committees

appropriations committees

budget committees

Congressional Budget Office (CBO)

Gramm-Rudman

Budget Enforcement Act (BEA)

mandatory spending

discretionary spending

entitlement

pay-as-you-go

Balanced Budget Act (BBA)

progressive taxation

incremental budgeting

uncontrollable outlay

social security

Social Security Act

Medicare

Medicaid

RESEARCH AND RESOURCES

1.   Which people make up issue networks and iron triangles? Who influences policymaking? What are their names? For whom do they work? If you are interested in finding answers to questions like these, you might turn to Arthur Close's *Washington Representatives* (Washington, D.C.: Columbia Books), an annual directory that lists lobbyists, consultants, legal advisers, foreign agents, and public affairs and government relations representatives. This work describes the clients handled by each representative, giving areas of interest and expertise, party affiliation, and ideological orientation. The volume also contains a list of organizations represented in Washington. Finally, it includes a list of selected topics, cross-referenced so that you may find out what companies or associations are likely to be active in what sort of policy discussions.

2.   Almost every American is affected by the public policies described in this chapter. The programs themselves were created by acts of Congress, but as you learned in Chapters 9 and 10, Congress does not specify every detail concerning every program. Instead, Congress leaves a considerable amount of discretion to the agencies charged with administering programs. These agencies make rules and establish procedures. But how can a citizen find out what the rules are? They are published in a government publication called the *Federal Register*. The *Federal Register* is now available on-line in a searchable form at <http://www.gpoaccess.gov/fr/index.html>.

The *Federal Register* is published daily. It includes "notices of proposed rule making," that is, agency proposals for new rules; these must be publicized before they can be implemented. When a proposed rule is adopted by an agency, it must be published again as a "final rule." Federal rules undergo constant revision. Each year, the rules of all the agencies are collected into a set of volumes called the *Code of Federal Regulations* (CFR). The CFR assigns "title numbers" to broad subject areas affected by regulatory action; for example, Title 7 deals with agriculture, and Title 45 deals with public welfare. Each title is broken down into chapters (designated by Roman numerals), and the chapters are further subdivided into numbered parts. For example, the rules and regulations of the Drug Enforcement Administration would be found in Title 21, Chapter XIII, Parts 1300-1399. The CFR is available on-line at <http://www.gpoaccess.gov/cfr/index.html>.

Two good on-line starting points in the hunt for government documents are GPO Access at <http://www.gpoaccess.gov/databases.html>, which allows searching multiple databases, and the documents center at the University of Michigan at <http://www.lib.umich.edu/govdocs/index.html>.

3. To see exactly what the government debt is on a given day, visit the Bureau of the Public Debt on-line at <http://www.publicdebt.treas.gov/opd/opdpdodt.htm>. This office reports what the government owes, updated each day to the penny.

USING YOUR KNOWLEDGE

1. What kind of groups takes an interest in sugar production? Compare this list with those groups that lobby for women's issues. Which issue (if either) would seem more likely to produce the kind of subsystem described as an iron triangle? Why?

2. Using the sites recommended above, track down a government document that provides information on either NATO expansion or tax reform.

3. A major concern of the text is political values. As this chapter indicates, two important sources of information about the values of a society are its tax code and its government's budget. The taxing and spending policies of a nation give people incentives to do some things but not others. To gain insight into American values, do one of the following:

    *   Obtain a copy of the filing instructions for the federal income tax. (The IRS publication *Your Federal Income Tax* covers personal income tax and is usually the most readily available, but you might want to look at tax laws for small businesses, farms, and so on. You can find IRS forms on-line at <http://www.irs.ustreas.gov/formspubs/index.html>.) Page through and look at the deductions allowed. What activities does the tax code seem to encourage? Do these tax regulations seem more likely to be the result of majoritarian or pluralist politics?

    *   Obtain a copy of the *Budget of the United States Government* from <http://www.whitehouse.gov/omb/>. Look through and examine the spending categories and the kinds of activities the government funds. Do these expenditures seem more likely to be the result of majoritarian or pluralist politics? Why?

SAMPLE EXAM QUESTIONS

Multiple-Choice Questions

1. A general plan of action used by a government to solve a social problem is called
    a.   feedback.
    b.   public policy.
    c.   oversight.
    d.   implementation.

2. Government policies that transfer resources from one segment of the public to another to foster equality are
    a.   distributive policies.
    b.   redistributional policies.
    c.   regulations.
    d.   impoundments.

3. Government policies that allocate funding for projects like building a highway are called

    a. distributive policies.
    b. redistributional policies.
    c. regulations.
    d. impoundments.

4. The term coined to refer to a small, tightly knit subsystem that includes congressional committee leaders, top agency personnel, and lobbyists is

    a. iron triangle.
    b. boondoggle.
    c. in-and-outer.
    d. issue network.

5. The increase in interest groups and congressional subcommittees has

    a. increased the power of iron triangles.
    b. closed the policymaking process.
    c. led political scientists to think of these subsystems as issue networks rather than iron triangles.
    d. reduced the requirement that subsystem participants possess technical expertise.

6. How does the government discover whether or not a policy is working?

    a. Through agenda setting
    b. Through policy formulation
    c. Through implementation
    d. Through policy evaluation

7. The stage of the policymaking process in which new issues are identified as problems to be addressed by government is called

    a. agenda setting.
    b. policy formulation.
    c. implementation.
    d. policy evaluation.

8. The part of the policymaking process concerned with carrying out policy is called

    a. agenda setting.
    b. policy formulation.
    c. implementation.
    d. policy evaluation.

9. Information received by policymakers about the effectiveness of public policy is called

    a. return.
    b. blowback.
    c. feedback.
    d. evaluation.

10. Cutting or increasing government spending to control business cycles is an example of the use of

    a. monetarism.
    b. fiscal policies.
    c. laissez faire.
    d. deficit financing.

11. Issue networks are generally

    a. broader than iron triangles.
    b. based upon shared policy expertise.
    c. encouraged by the career paths of in-and-outers.
    d. All of the above.

12. A tax system that requires wealthier people to pay a higher percentage of their income in taxes is known as

    a. regressive.
    b. progressive.
    c. revenue-neutral.
    d. flat.

13. Tax policy has been used to

    a. raise revenue to fund the government.
    b. promote greater equality among taxpayers.
    c. control the economy.
    d. All of the above.

14. The traditional two-step budget process of authorization and appropriation offered rich opportunities for the practice of

    a. majoritarian democracy.
    b. pluralist democracy.
    c. presidential power.
    d. judicial review.

15. Which of the following congressional committees are involved in budgeting?

    a. Tax committees
    b. Authorization committees
    c. Appropriations committees
    d. All of the above

16. When agencies draft a budget asking for the amount they received in the current year plus an additional amount for new programs, they are engaged in

    a. incremental budgeting.
    b. discretionary spending.
    c. mandatory spending.
    d. zero-based budgeting.

17. "Uncontrollable" programs are immune to budget cutting because

    a. Congress has passed legislation entitling individuals to a certain level of benefits.
    b. powerful political groups act to pressure Congress against cuts in pet entitlement programs.
    c. the government has assumed financial obligations and responsibilities it must meet (for example, paying interest on its debts).
    d. All of the above.

18. Social security is an example of

    a. an entitlement program.
    b. a "pay-as-you-go" program.
    c. a compulsory insurance program.
    d. All of the above.

19. Gramm-Rudman was an attempt to

    a. shore up the Social Security Trust Fund.
    b. eliminate poverty.
    c. cut the deficit.
    d. increase taxes without public awareness.

20. Social security is called a pay-as-you-go system, which means that

    a. today's workers support today's elderly.
    b. you pay in while you are working, and the money is saved until you go on pension.
    c. it is a progressive tax.
    d. it is financed by income taxes.

Essay Questions

1. Explain the four key stages of the policymaking process.

2. Discuss whether the growth of issue networks made the United States more or less democratic.

3. Outline the process of passing the federal budget, explaining the roles of the key institutional players.

4. Explain the difference between entitlements and discretionary spending, giving concrete examples of each type of outlay.

5. Explain why the Social Security program faces severe economic challenges in the future. Discuss options to rescue the system.

ANSWERS TO MULTIPLE-CHOICE QUESTIONS

1. b
2. b
3. a
4. a
5. c
6. d
7. a
8. c
9. c
10. b
11. d
12. b
13. d
14. b
15. d
16. a
17. d
18. d
19. c
20. a